# THE BIBLE OLYMPICS

## BOB PHILLIPS

HARVEST
HOUSE
PUBLISHERS
Eugene, Oregon 97402

**Bible Olympics**

Copyright © 1995 by Harvest House Publishers
Eugene, Oregon 97402

ISBN 1-56507-296-7

**Printed in the United States of America.**

# Introduction

**I**n our fast-paced society we often do not take time to have fun. Sometimes we even feel guilty when we take a moment to relax. When was the last time you slowed down and got your mind off the pressures of a busy life? When was the last time you treated yourself to a mini-vacation?

Bible Olympics is designed to provide many hours of satisfying entertainment, growth, and learning. It will give you bite-sized escapes to refresh your mind and spirit. You'll get a big kick out of coming up with solutions to the:

- **Word Hunts**
- **Versigrams**
- **Tail Tags**
- **Patchword Puzzles**
- **Anagrams**
- **Jumbles**
- **Impossible Mazes**
- **Bible Riddles**
- **and much more**

You can sharpen your skills, test your Bible knowledge, and challenge your mind all at the same time. You may like to use some of the puzzles with your family as a mealtime diversion or as a method of learning while traveling by car. Some of the games and riddles lend themselves to a group challenge at a Bible study or Sunday school class. You may want to share Bible Olympics with a shut-in or someone who's in the hospital. Try sending a copy to a missionary friend as a change of pace.

Some of the puzzles are easy and some are more difficult. It wouldn't be fun if they were too easy. So jump right in to whatever catches your fancy.

Have a great time. If you get stuck, the answers are in the back of the book. You can peek if you want to—no one will be watching.

We hope you won't struggle too much—just enough to experience the joy of learning and the satisfaction of solving a problem through your own resourcefulness. If you like these puzzles and have some of your own ingenious variations that you think other people would enjoy, drop us a note and include them.*

**Bob Phillips**
Hume, California

*Bible puzzles, riddles, and games—along with clean jokes— can be mailed to:

**Family Services**
**P.O. Box 9363**
**Fresno, CA 93792**

# Name the Event

The picture below illustrates a Bible event, story, or verse. See if you can guess which Bible event, story, or verse the picture is illustrating.

_____

_____

_____

_____

_____

Where in the Bible is this event, story, or verse found?

_____

_____

# Old Testament Time, Quantity, and Number

1. _____How many years did God provide manna for the children of Israel in the wilderness?

2. _____How many priests with trumpets marched around the city of Jericho?

3. _____How many "cities of refuge" were there?

4. _____How many days did Samson give his 30 companions to solve his riddle?

5. _____How many men and women were killed in the fall of the building that was pulled down by Samson?

6. _____How old was David when he died?

7. _____How long did it take Solomon to build the temple?

8. _____How many times did the Shunammite woman's son sneeze when he was coming to life?

9. _____How many days did it take Nehemiah to rebuild the walls of Jerusalem?

10. _____How many sons of Haman were hanged?

11. _____How many things does Solomon say the Lord hates?

12. _____How long were the Jews in captivity in Babylon?

13. _____How many years did Nebuchadnezzar eat grass like an ox?

14. _____How many weeks were allotted in Daniel's dream for the finishing of transgression?

15. _____How long were the Ninevites given to repent?

A. 7 years

B. 6

C. 10

D. 40

E. 70 weeks

F. 52 days

G. 70 years

H. 7

I. 40 days

J. 3000

K. 7 things

L. 7 times

M. 7 days

# Runaway

In eight moves, see if you can discover the name of a runaway slave. Paul pled for forgiveness for this runaway slave
in Philemon 10-12.

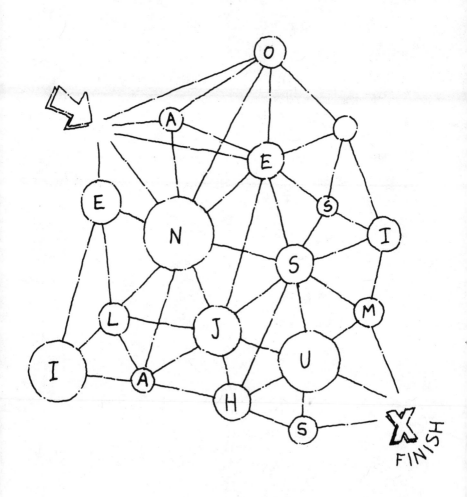

# Key Word

To find the key word, fill in the blanks in words 1 through 10 with the correct missing letters. Transfer those letters to the correspondingly numbered squares in the diagram.

1. ( )RK
2. GRAI( )
3. BE( )HEL
4. BR( )CK
5. ( )REED

6. TOOT( )
7. CA( )TS
8. ( )VORY
9. BEA( )T
10. A( )ONE

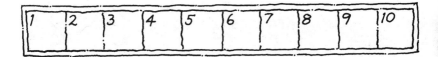

| 1 | 2 | 3 | 4 | 5 | 6 | 7 | 8 | 9 | 10 |
|---|---|---|---|---|---|---|---|---|----|

# Solomon's Treasure

See if you can find your way through the maze of open doors. It will lead you to Solomon's treasure.

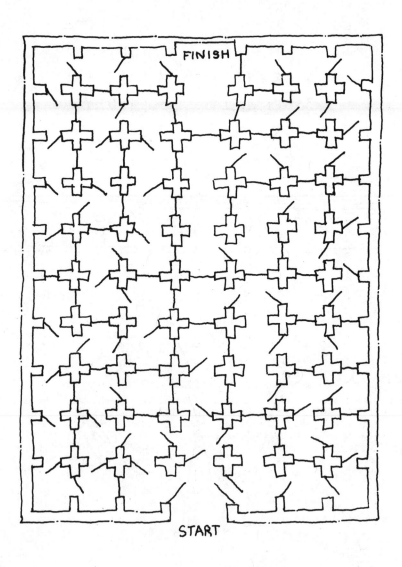

FINISH

START

# The Attributes of God

See if you can discover 23 of the attributes of God in this word search puzzle.

Benevolent      Good          Light          Spirit

Creator         Holy          Omnipresent    Sustainer

Deliverer       Immutable     Omniscient     Trinity

Eternal         Just          Omnipotent     Truth

Forgiving       Kind          Righteous      Unity

Gentle          Life          Sovereign

```
T O G J C R E A T O R T Y D I
S R M O U V Y G P T H T N S M
O T U N O S D J N G I I O U M
V R I T I D T E I N K A S S U
E I U O H P L L U Z V A C T T
R N A H Y O R S C Z C O Q A A
E I R V V E D E P D Z Y G I B
I T P E L Y F E S I B S D N L
G Y N T L B U X L E R L A E E
N E N O V G F U D I N I I R N
B E H E T E R N A L V T T F G
G R I G H T E O U S N E J H E
D O C F O R G I V I N G R U Z
O M N I S C I E N T M W Q E T
O M N I P O T E N T F M Z Y R
```

# Quotation Puzzle

In the puzzle below, fit the letters of each column into the boxes directly above them. The letters may or may not go into the boxes in the same order in which they are listed. It is up to you to decide which letter goes into which box. Once a letter is used, cross it off the bottom half of the diagram and do not use it again. The letter H has been entered into a box to help you get started, and that letter has been crossed off. Black squares are used to separate the words of the quotation. When the diagram is filled in, you will find the completed quotation by reading the boxes horizontally.

| H | | | | | | | | | | | | | | | | | |

| H | R | N | I | R | T | T | E | D | L | T | D | O | R | I | F | E | R |
| B | U | F | O | G | I | H | E | A | A | N | H | | L | F | D | A | |
| | O | M | N | L | | A | Y | | | | L | | A | D | E | | |
| | O | I | | | | W | N | | | | | | | N | | | |

# New Testament Questions

1. ____How many petitions are recorded in the Lord's Prayer?

2. ____How many baskets of fragments were gathered after feeding the 4000?

3. ____How often did the Mosaic law say a man should forgive his brother?

4. ____How often did Jesus say you should forgive an offending brother?

5. ____When shall the whole human race see Jesus on His throne?

6. ____How long was darkness over the land when Jesus was crucified?

7. ____How many swine were driven into the sea by Jesus?

8. ____How long was Jesus hanging on the cross?

9. ____How long did Anna live with her husband?

10. ____What is the longest drought recorded in the Bible?

A. 70 times 7

B. 6 hours

C. 7 baskets

D. 3 1/2 years

E. 6

F. 2000

G. 7 times

H. 3 hours

I. At the judgment

J. 7 years

# Who Said It?

All of the following quotes were said or written by one of the following individuals. See if you can guess "Who said it?"

### Agur/Daniel/David/Esther/Gideon
### Job/Joshua/Isaiah/Micah/Solomon

1. "Your teeth are like a flock of sheep."

   _____

2. "Do not let this Book of the Law depart from your mouth."

   _____

3. "Whom shall I send? And who will go for us?"

   _____

4. "If I have found favor with you..."

   _____

5. "But you, Bethlehem Ephrathah, though you are small among the clans of Judah..."

   _____

6. "Do not be angry with me. Let me make just one more request."

   _____

7. "He who dwells in the shelter of the Most High will rest in the shadow of the Almighty."

_____

8. "A lizard can be caught with the hand, yet it is found in kings' palaces."

_____

9. "If you can read this writing and tell me what it means, you will be clothed in purple and have a gold chain placed around your neck."

_____

10. "The fear of the Lord—that is wisdom, and to shun evil is understanding."

_____

# Bible Labyrinth

Hidden in the following Bible labyrinth is a verse from the Bible. Start with the entry arrow and move one space at a time to the right, left, up, or down. You should finish the verse at the exit arrow.

| A | P | L | E | A | S | E | B | A | C | C | E | P | T | Z |
|---|---|---|---|---|---|---|---|---|---|---|---|---|---|---|
| L | | M | | B | | V | | U | | S | | A | | A |
| S | N | E | F | F | O | W | M | O | C | O | H | W | E | H |
| E | | N | | O | | C | | V | | B | | X | | T |
| P | R | O | P | N | L | O | V | E | D | H | E | M | Y | H |
| D | | M | | A | | C | | R | | T | | A | | E |
| E | T | O | Q | R | E | V | O | S | L | S | E | T | C | L |
| S | | N | | D | | O | | P | | T | | T | | O |
| L | O | V | E | E | K | R | E | P | E | A | R | E | F | R |
| C | | E | | E | | R | | T | | Q | | R | | D |
| H | Z | B | R | F | J | E | F | R | A | P | E | S | G | G |
| R | | U | | Y | | V | | A | | G | | H | | H |
| I | X | T | W | H | O | E | I | T | E | S | C | L | O | S |
| S | | W | | S | | J | | T | | U | | V | | E |
| T | T | O | O | A | Y | K | I | S | D | N | E | I | R | F |

# Patchword

This patchwork-quilt diagram contains 15 Bible words or names all mixed up. Two patches form one word—use each patch only once. See if you can piece together the names and words and write them on the lines below.

1. _____    6. _____    11. _____

2. _____    7. _____    12. _____

3. _____    8. _____    13. _____

4. _____    9. _____    14. _____

5. _____    10. _____   15. _____

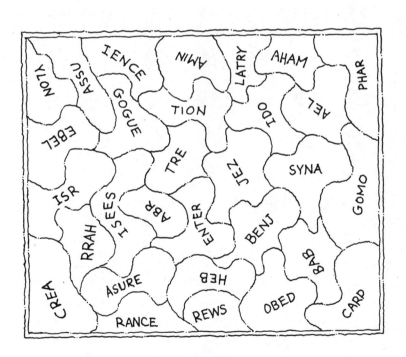

# Jumbles

For both of the jumbles below, unscramble the names of four men mentioned in the Bible. Write these names on the blanks to the right. The letters in the parentheses now form a new scrambled name. Write these letters on the blanks provided. Now unscramble this name.

SCRAMBLED NAME    UNSCRAMBLED NAME

1. KODAZ    ( ) __ __ __ __

   NIMJABEN    ( ) ( ) __ __ __ __ __ __

   GOABNEED    __ __ ( ) __ __ ( ) __ __

   EDSMA    ( ) ( ) __ __ __

   New scrambled name    ( ) ( ) ( ) ( ) ( ) ( ) ( )

   Unscrambled name    __ __ __ __ __ __ __

2. HHAAORP    ( ) __ ( ) __ __ __ ( )

   SUITT    __ ( ) ( ) __ __

   PZORAH    __ __ ( ) __ __ ( )

   DOBE    ( ) __ __ __

   New scrambled name    ( ) ( ) ( ) ( ) ( ) ( ) ( ) ( )

   Unscrambled name    __ __ __ __ __ __ __ __

# Paul's Puzzle

Help Paul solve this puzzle by placing the 12 boxes, each containing one or two letters, into the empty diagram below. The puzzle will form four Bible names reading across and down, as shown in the small puzzle to the left. There are three men's names and one woman's name.

# Humorous Bible Riddles

1. What are two of the smallest insects mentioned in the Bible?

   _____

2. Who is the smallest man mentioned in the Bible?

   _____

3. One of the first things Cain did after he left the Garden of Eden was to take a nap. How do we know this?

   _____

4. Where is the second math problem mentioned in the Bible?

   _____

5. Where is the first math problem mentioned in the Bible?

   _____

6. If Methuselah was the oldest man in the Bible (969 years of age), why did he die before his father?

   _____

7. Was there any money on Noah's ark?

   _____

8. Where in the Bible does it say that fathers should let their sons use the automobile?

_____

9. Where does it talk about Honda cars in the Bible?

_____

10. What prophet in the Bible was a space traveler?

_____

# Versigram

See if you can unscramble the following familiar Bible verses.

1. eB gnayr, nda tye od tno nis; od tno elt hte nsu og wodn no uryo ganre.

   _____

   _____

2. uBt sdgonilse ltucalya si a amesn fo rgate inga, nhew ocmpcandiae yb tcnotennmte.

   _____

   _____

3. bvAeo lal, ekpe vfrente ni uyor vleo ofr noe nhaorte, uebcaes vloe vcorse a etmudulti fo niss.

   _____

   _____

4. rheTe si on afer ni ovel; btu recptfe vleo scast tuo afre, scubeae afre vionlsve shpnuimten, nad het neo hwo safer si tno ftecdeper ni olev.

   _____

   _____

5. oD otn frae hwta uoy rae buato ot fsfure. ehBodl, het veidl si uboat ot sact mose fo ouy otni irpsno, htta ouy yam eb stdete, nad uoy iwil vhea oubltnirtai etn ydsa. eB hftialfu nltui aehtd, dna I lwil vgei ouy hte wrcno fo file.

   _____

   _____

**18**

# Fuzzy Thinking

See if you can find your way through the maze of fuzzy thinking and discover good thoughts.

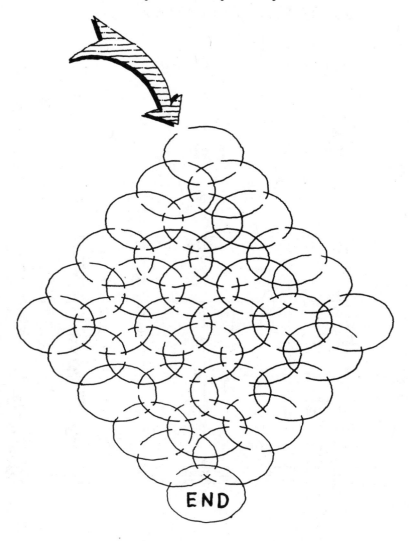

END

# Alphanumber

In the diagram below there are various numbers in the squares. The numbers represent letters of the alphabet. Change the numbers to letters and discover an important Bible thought.

| A | B | C | D | E | F | G | H | I | J | K | L | M | N |
|---|---|---|---|---|---|---|---|---|---|---|---|---|---|
| 1 | 2 | 3 | 4 | 5 | 6 | 7 | 8 | 9 | 10 | 11 | 12 | 13 | 14 |

| O | P | Q | R | S | T | U | V | W | X | Y | Z |
|---|---|---|---|---|---|---|---|---|---|---|---|
| 15 | 16 | 17 | 18 | 19 | 20 | 21 | 22 | 23 | 24 | 25 | 26 | 27 |

| 4 | 5 | 12 | 9 | 7 | 8 | 20 | 27 | 25 | 15 | 21 | 18 |
|---|---|---|---|---|---|---|---|---|---|---|---|
| 19 | 5 | 12 | 6 | 27 | 9 | 14 | 27 | 20 | 8 | 5 | 27 |
| 27 | 12 | 15 | 18 | 4 | 27 | 1 | 14 | 4 | 27 | 8 | 5 |
| 23 | 9 | 12 | 12 | 27 | 27 | 7 | 9 | 22 | 5 | 27 | 27 |
| 24 | 25 | 15 | 21 | 27 | 20 | 8 | 5 | 27 | 27 | 4 | 5 |
| 19 | 9 | 18 | 5 | 19 | 27 | 27 | 15 | 6 | 27 | 27 | 27 |
| 27 | 25 | 15 | 21 | 18 | 27 | 27 | 8 | 5 | 1 | 18 | 20 |

# Priscilla's Problem

Help Priscilla place the lettered pieces into the empty diagram below. If placed correctly, 20 five-lettered words will be formed. The words can be read by reading across the tops and bottoms of the pieces, and by reading down the left and right sides of the pieces. The arrows indicate where each word begins.

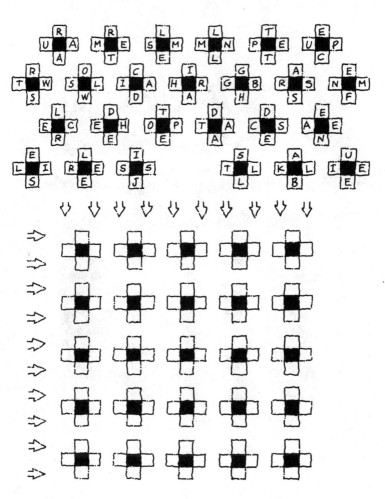

# Something You Should Be

Unscramble the mixed-up word below and see if you can
discover something that you should always be.

# Tail Tag

Begin at the top arrow and find a verse from the Bible.
Move one square at a time to the right, left, up, down, or
diagonally. End the verse at the side arrow.

| A | D | O | T | S | Y | O | U | F | H | E | N | J | O | Y | G | L |
|---|---|---|---|---|---|---|---|---|---|---|---|---|---|---|---|---|
| I | E | I | R | H | J | D | O | I | N | G |   | W | H | U | M | W |
| K | Q | M | J | P | E | Y | A | Z | U | R | E | K | A | O | L | F |
| L | T | H | E | O | H | E | A | N | C | K |   | J | U | B | C | A |
| I | B | Y | O | U | D | X | R | C | D | D | B | I | B | L | E | N |
| K | L | I | E | C | Z | L | T | S | N | Y | N | E | E | D | Z | U |
| E | T | M | F | E | D | S | I | T | O | O | T | E | R | E | D | N |
| O | F | W | O | L | Y | M | P | I | C | S | Y | E | S | K | I | Z |
| N | P | U | A | C | L | E | P | T | D | B | E | M | T | Y | J | X |
| T | B | Q | L | C | H | R | I | S | N | T | W | I | X | A | S | D |
| O | F | C | G | A | G | U | H | T | A | R | Y | O | U | R | N | D |
| P | H | P | B | H | O | N | G | S | W | U | X |   | I | X | I | C |
| M | V | O | Q | Q | W | I | D | P | U | Z | Z | E | L | S | B | T |
| A | V | C | B | R | T | H | U | S | A | V | I | O | U | R | G | Y |
| K | D | E | A | L | L | R | P | R | A | I | S | E | F | N | U | A |
| E | E | O | T | M | E | S | E | O | I | F | F | E | R | E | N | T |
| S | G | A | M | E | S | A | T | F | O | R | T |   | Y | O | U | Z |

# Name the Event

The picture below illustrates a Bible event, story, or verse. See if you can guess which Bible event, story, or verse the picture is illustrating.

_____

_____

_____

_____

_____

Where in the Bible is this event, story, or verse found?

_____

_____

# Quotation Puzzle

In the puzzle below, fit the letters of each column into the boxes directly above them. The letters may or may not go into the boxes in the same order in which they are listed. It is up to you to decide which letter goes into which box. Once a letter is used, cross it off the bottom half of the diagram and do not use it again. Some letters have been entered into boxes to help you get started, and those letters have been crossed off. Black squares are used to separate the words of the quotation. When the diagram is filled in, you will find the completed quotation by reading the boxes horizontally.

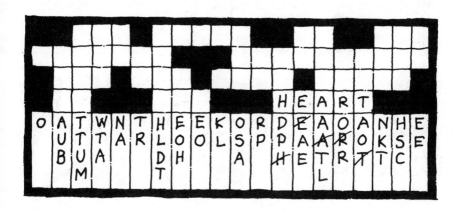

# Wrestling with a Lion

In seven moves, see if you can discover who killed a lion in a pit on a snowy day. The story is found in 1 Chronicles 11:22.

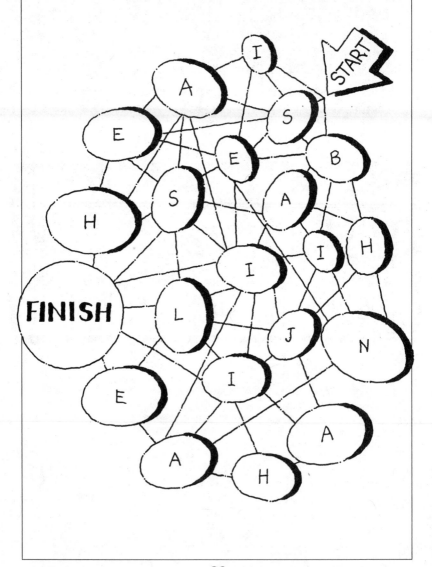

# Odd or Even

To discover this important Bible message, cross out the letters above all the odd numbers.

| E | P | I | S | R | M | A | I | E |
|---|---|---|---|---|---|---|---|---|
| 17 | 24 | 11 | 19 | 32 | 63 | 8 | 14 | 23 |
| N | S | S | E | S | A | T | F | H |
| 71 | 52 | 57 | 60 | 45 | 41 | 22 | 59 | 16 |
| B | E | R | L | I | O | S | R | D |
| 13 | 80 | 7 | 48 | 83 | 68 | 23 | 4 | 36 |

# 12 Things That Happen at Salvation

See if you can discover 12 things that happen at the moment of salvation.

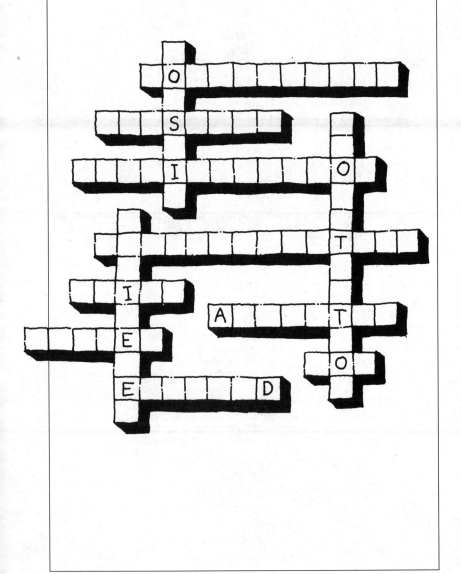

# Old Testament Sprint

See if you can sprint through the Old Testament and
identify 12 Old Testament books. Letters have been placed
in the tracks to give you a head start.

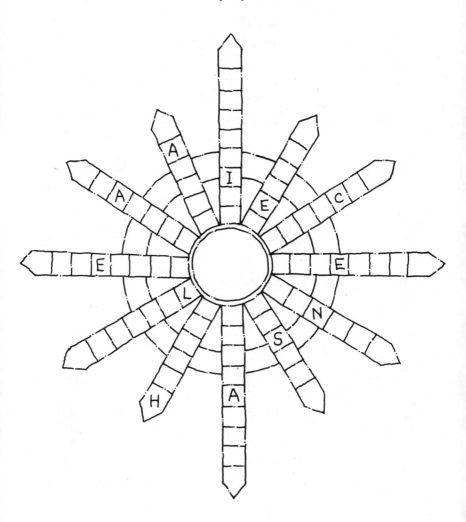

# Famous People Search

Can you find the following names in the puzzle below?

| | | | | |
|---|---|---|---|---|
| Aaron | Cain | Ezra | James | Luke |
| Abel | Daniel | Felix | Job | Mark |
| Abraham | David | Gideon | John | Naaman |
| Absalom | Elijah | Goliath | Jonah | Pharaoh |
| Achan | Elisha | Herod | Joseph | Samson |
| Adam | Enoch | Isaac | Joshua | Thomas |
| Amos | Esau | Isaiah | Judas | |
| Barnabas | Ezekiel | Jacob | Lazarus | |

```
S  A  A  M  T  H  O  M  A  S  S  A  H  H  M
E  B  B  C  A  J  O  H  N  O  A  P  A  O  S
E  Z  A  R  H  D  M  D  M  R  E  J  L  M  X
C  N  E  R  A  A  A  A  O  S  I  A  Z  I  P
J  A  O  K  N  H  N  N  O  L  S  A  L  S  H
A  K  I  C  I  A  A  J  E  B  C  E  J  A  A
M  R  O  N  H  E  B  M  A  C  F  T  O  D  R
E  A  A  U  D  N  L  A  H  A  H  E  B  U  A
S  M  A  I  A  G  H  A  S  D  U  E  Z  J  O
K  S  V  M  I  T  E  N  I  A  A  H  R  R  H
E  A  A  D  A  U  J  I  O  S  H  N  S  O  A
D  A  E  I  A  O  Z  Q  S  S  A  S  I  O  D
N  O  L  B  N  L  U  K  E  A  M  I  I  E  J
N  O  E  A  D  B  O  C  A  J  A  A  A  L  L
G  L  H  L  A  Z  A  R  U  S  U  C  S  H  E
```

# A Special Blessing

See if you can unroll the scroll and complete each of the sentences.
Find the special blessing mentioned in Psalm 1:1-3 (NASB).

HOW BLESSED IS
IN THE COUNSE
NOR STAND I
NOR SIT IN
BUT HIS DEL
AND IN HIS L
AND HE WILL
FIRMLY PLAN
WHICH YIELD
AND ITS LEA
AND IN WHAT

# Odd or Even

To discover this important Bible event, cross out the
letters above all the odd numbers.

| E | L | N | I | O | J | C | A | H |
|---|---|---|---|---|---|---|---|---|
| 14 | 17 | 2 | 1 | 64 | 39 | 72 | 73 | 10 |
| R | W | A | A | L | I | K | S | S |
| 41 | 24 | 89 | 52 | 46 | 27 | 4 | 36 | 11 |
| W | E | I | T | H | S | G | O | D |
| 8 | 93 | 22 | 12 | 38 | 81 | 94 | 18 | 66 |

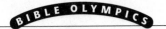

# Help Pharaoh

See if you can help Pharaoh find his way back to the center
of the pyramid.

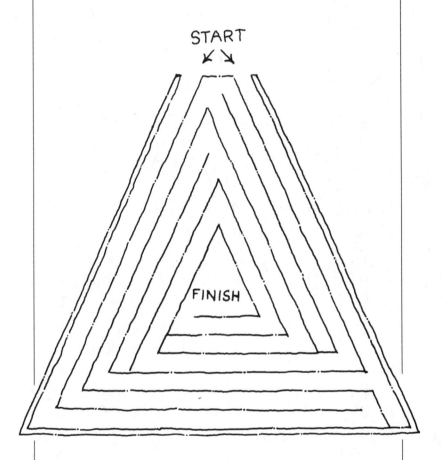

# Dodo's Dilemma

There are three men named Dodo in the Old Testament. How many separate times is the name Dodo used in this puzzle? How many "D's" are
in the puzzle? How many "O's" are in the puzzle?

Number of Dodo's _____

Number of "D's" _____

Number of "O's" _____

```
O D O D O D O D O D O D O D O
D O D O D O D O D O D O D O D
O D O D O D O D O D O D O D O
D O D O D O D O D O D O D O D
O D O D O D O D O D O D O D O
D O D O D O D O D O D O D O D
O D O D O D O D O D O D O D O
D O D O D O D O D O D O D O D
O D O D O D O D O D O D O D O
D O D O D O D O D O D O D O D
O D O D O D O D O D O D O D O
D O D O D O D O D O D O D O D
O D O D O D O D O D O D O D O
D O D O D O D O D O D O D O D
O D O D O D O D O D O D O D O
D O D O D O D O D O D O D O D
O D O D O D O D O D O D O D O
```

34

# Name the Event

The picture below illustrates a Bible event, story, or verse. See if you can guess which Bible event, story, or verse the picture is illustrating.

_____

_____

_____

_____

_____

Where in the Bible is this event, story, or verse found?

_____

_____

# Win First Prize

You will win first prize if you can identify all the firsts mentioned in the Bible quiz below. Match the proper individual with the proper event.

1. _____ What was the first command?

2. _____ Who made the first clothing for man?

3. _____ Who built the first city?

4. _____ Who was the first bigamist on record?

5. _____ Who first used a saddle in the Bible?

6. _____ Who is the first woman whose age is mentioned?

7. _____ Who wore the first bridal veil?

8. _____ Who was the first judge in the Bible?

9. _____ Who was the first Jewish high priest?

10. _____ Who was the first man to be struck dead for lying?

11. _____ Who was the first woman to have leprosy?

12. _____ Who was the first to commit suicide?

13. _____ Who was the first raised from the dead?

14. _____ Who was the first Gentile convert?

15. _____ Who was the first woman to get a written recommendation from Paul?

A. Sarah

B. Ananias

C. Moses

D. Cain

E. Saul

F. "Let there be light"

G. Cornelius

H. Rebekah

I. Phoebe

J. Lamech

K. Miriam

L. God

M. Aaron

N. Abraham

O. The widow at Zarephath's son

# Nodding Off to Sleep

In four moves, see if you can discover the name of the man who slept in the land of Nod. The story is found in Genesis 4:16.

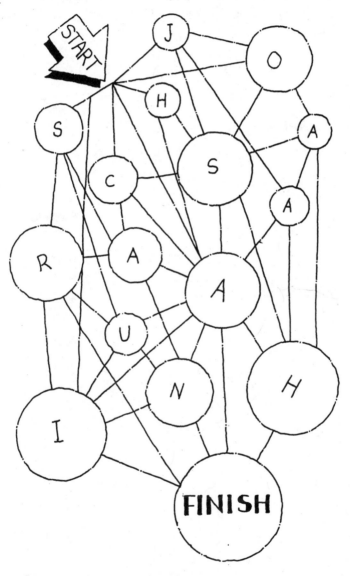

# Key Word

To find the key word, fill in the blanks in words 1 through 10 with the correct missing letters.  Transfer those letters to the correspondingly numbered squares in the diagram.

1. ( ) L O O D        6. ( ) I S D O M
2. R I V ( ) R        7. W I T N E ( ) S
3. D E V I ( )        8. S T O R E ( ) O U S E
4. B ( ) O O D        9. S A ( ) N T
5. L ( ) C U S T     10. R O ( ) E

| 1 | 2 | 3 | 4 | 5 | 6 | 7 | 8 | 9 | 10 |
|---|---|---|---|---|---|---|---|---|----|
|   |   |   |   |   |   |   |   |   |    |

# Quotation Puzzle

In the puzzle below, fit the letters of each column into the boxes directly above them. The letters may or may not go into the boxes in the same order in which they are listed. It is up to you to decide which letter goes into which box. Once a letter is used, cross it off the bottom half of the diagram and do not use it again. Some letters have been entered into boxes to help you get started, and those letters have been crossed off. Black squares are used to separate the words of the quotation. When the diagram is filled in, you will find the completed quotation by reading the boxes horizontally.

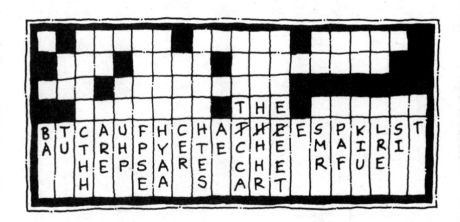

# Bible Labyrinth

Hidden in the following Bible labyrinth is a verse from the Bible. Start with the entry arrow and move one space at a time to the right, left, up, or down. You should finish the verse at the exit arrow.

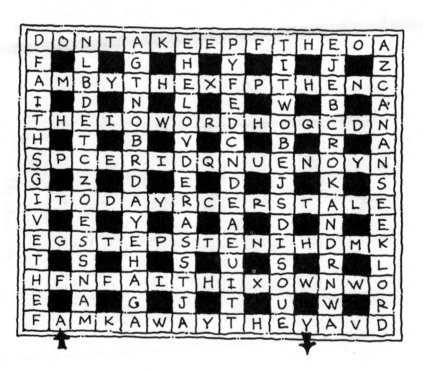

# Patchword

This patchwork-quilt diagram contains 15 Bible words or names all mixed up. Three patches form one word—use each patch only once. See if you can piece together the names and words and write them on the lines below.

1. _____   6. _____   11. _____

2. _____   7. _____   12. _____

3. _____   8. _____   13. _____

4. _____   9. _____   14. _____

5. _____   10. _____   15. _____

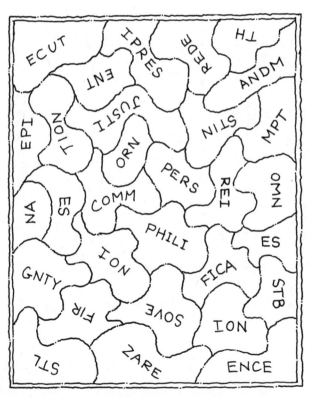

# Jumbles

For both of the jumbles below, unscramble the names of four women mentioned in the Bible. Write these names on the blanks to the right. The letters in the parentheses now form a new scrambled name. Write these letters on the blanks provided. Now unscramble this name.

SCRAMBLED NAME    UNSCRAMBLED NAME

1. POHAR          __ __ ( ) ( ) __

   IIRMMA         __ ( ) ( ) ( ) __ __

   OSLI           ( ) __ __ ( )

   CHJOEIAL       __ __ ( ) __ ( ) __ __ __

   New scrambled name   ( ) ( ) ( ) ( ) ( ) ( ) ( ) ( )

   Unscrambled name   __ __ __ __ __ __ __ __ __ __


2. LEBZEEJ        ( ) ( ) __ ( ) ( ) __ __

   SOARDC         ( ) __ __ ( ) __ __

   TVAIHS         __ __ __ ( ) __ __ ( )

   ONAMI          __ __ ( ) __ __

   New scrambled name   ( ) ( ) ( ) ( ) ( ) ( ) ( ) ( )

   Unscrambled name   __ __ __ __ __ __ __ __

# Name the Event

The picture below illustrates a Bible event, story, or verse. See if you can guess which Bible event, story, or verse the picture is illustrating.

_____

_____

_____

_____

_____

Where in the Bible is this event, story, or verse found?

_____

_____

# 28 Seasons

See if you can find the following 23 of the 28 seasons that are mentioned in Ecclesiastes, the third chapter (KJV).

| | | | |
|---|---|---|---|
| Break down | Hate | Lose | Rend |
| Build up | Heal | Love | Sew |
| Dance | Keep | Mourn | Speak |
| Die | Keep silence | Peace | War |
| Embrace | Kill | Plant | Weep |
| Get | Laugh | Pluck | |

```
E  P  D  I  E  G  Q  T  B  D  N  H
K  T  E  M  R  A  W  R  A  R  E  G
S  E  A  E  R  N  E  N  U  A  M  E
E  C  E  H  K  A  C  O  L  M  H  T
W  M  U  P  K  E  M  P  E  F  H  W
C  Z  O  D  S  P  G  P  L  S  U  V
P  Y  O  K  P  I  U  H  E  U  O  N
Q  W  I  L  K  R  L  D  G  A  C  L
N  L  A  A  E  P  E  E  L  U  C  K
L  N  E  V  E  X  U  N  N  I  A  E
T  P  O  E  X  U  S  Z  D  C  U  L
S  L  W  E  C  A  R  B  M  E  E  B
```

# A Quote from John

Start at the arrow and move one square at a time in any direction. You may move to the right, left, up, down, or diagonally, but do not cross any letter twice. All letters must be used to discover the quote from John, found in 1 John 3:24.

| T | E | S | N | D | L | I | E |
|---|---|---|---|---|---|---|---|
| W | H | O | A | M | S | I | V |
| H | B | Y | H | I | M | N | H |
| O | O | E | S | C | O | I | M |
|   |   | E | N | T | D | N | A |
|   | M | H | I | E | H |   |   |

# Humorous Bible Riddles

1. What has God never seen, Abraham Lincoln seldom saw, and a man today sees every day?

_____

2. Where does it say in the Bible that we should not fly in airplanes?

_____

3. Where in the Bible does it talk about smoking?

_____

4. What was the name of Isaiah's horse?

_____

5. What do you have that Cain, Abel, and Seth never had?

_____

6. Why do you think that the kangaroo was the most miserable animal on the Ark?

_____

7. What simple affliction brought about the death of Samson?

_____

8. How were the Egyptians paid for goods taken by the Israelites when they fled from Egypt?

_____

9. Where in the Bible does it suggest that men should wash dishes?

_____

10. Paul the apostle was a great preacher and teacher and earned his living as a tentmaker. What other occupation did Paul have?

_____

# Odd or Even

To discover this important Bible event, cross out the letters above all the odd numbers.

| C | B | R | A | E | P | A | T | T |
|---|---|---|---|---|---|---|---|---|
| 17 | 12 | 11 | 32 | 27 | 4 | 53 | 97 | 22 |
| I | L | S | O | M | V | E | O | F |
| 74 | 9 | 8 | 51 | 66 | 87 | 33 | 38 | 92 |
| J | C | E | R | S | I | E | U | S |
| 8 | 9 | 26 | 35 | 44 | 47 | 73 | 56 | 62 |

# Square Deal

In dealing with others we should always give them a "square deal"
(being fair and honest). See if you can find your way through the maze
to your square deal.

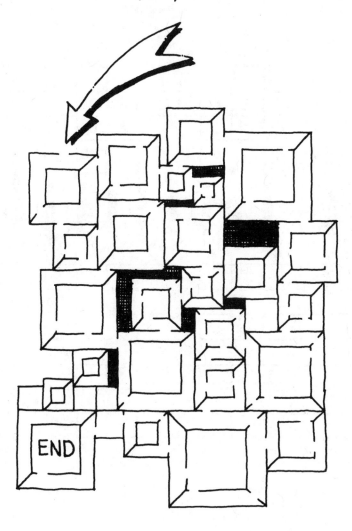

# Bible Women

The letters in the following columns go into the boxes directly below them, but in different order.  When the letters are correctly placed they will spell the names of eight Bible women.  See if you can discover who these Bible women are.

| M | I | R | A | B | I | L | Y | U | I | H | L |
|---|---|---|---|---|---|---|---|---|---|---|---|
| E | V | H | I | D | M | R | R | C | T | E |   |
| N | A | O | M | I |   | N | A | D | H | A |   |
| R | A | E | A |   | A |   | H |   |   |   |   |

# A Place for Everyone

Can you find a place for every one of the five-lettered names of Bible characters listed below? Three individuals have already been given a place.

| | | | | |
|---|---|---|---|---|
| Abner | Eliab | Herod | Jesse | Peter |
| Amasa | Elias | Hosea | Jobab | Rufus |
| Annas | Felix | Isaac | Jonah | Sheba |
| Caleb | Gaius | Ittai | Micah | Simon |
| David | Gomer | Jacob | Moses | Titus |
| Demas | Haman | James | Nabal | Uriah |

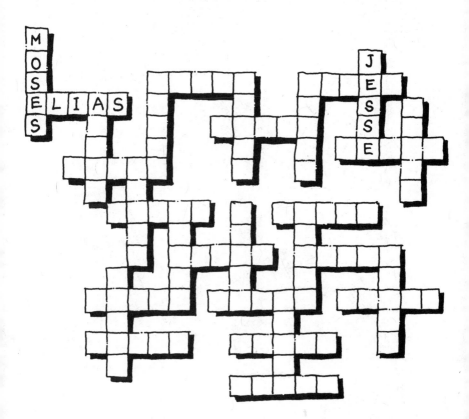

# Extra Days

In seven moves, see if you can discover how many years were added to
Hezekiah's life. The story is found in 2 Kings 20:5-7.

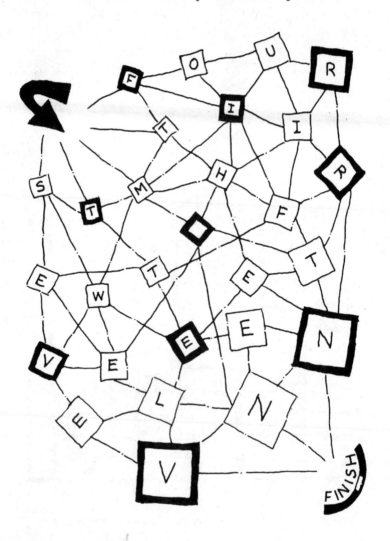

# Animals, Birds, & Reptiles

See how many of the animals, birds, and reptiles of the Bible you can find in the puzzle below.

| | | | | |
|---|---|---|---|---|
| Apes | Cow | Goat | Mouse | Sheep |
| Badger | Deer | Hawk | Ostrich | Snake |
| Bats | Dog | Horse | Owl | Sparrow |
| Bears | Dove | Lamb | Pig | Tortoise |
| Boar | Eagle | Leopard | Quail | Weasel |
| Camel | Fish | Lion | Rabbit | Wolf |
| Chicken | Fox | Lizard | Raven | |

```
H  C  L  A  W  O  L  F  T  N  R  E  T  D
W  C  A  I  P  V  L  W  O  E  A  I  R  E
L  E  I  M  A  E  F  O  E  G  B  A  E  N
S  A  A  R  E  U  S  D  L  B  P  S  E  C
P  Q  M  S  T  L  Q  E  A  O  I  V  P  O
A  L  M  B  E  S  L  R  E  O  A  P  I  W
R  X  J  K  F  L  O  L  T  R  D  G  G  Y
R  O  E  I  E  B  N  R  H  S  R  O  E  Q
O  F  S  S  E  R  O  E  D  O  H  A  V  Q
W  H  U  A  E  T  S  D  K  R  R  E  O  E
F  O  R  G  B  N  K  F  T  C  A  S  E  B
M  S  D  A  A  W  H  L  M  A  I  Z  E  P
K  A  T  K  A  D  O  G  N  T  O  H  I  U
B  S  E  H  B  D  I  N  O  I  L  G  C  L
```

# Help the Ants

Help the ants of Proverbs prepare for the winter. Can you direct them back home to where the baby ants are living?

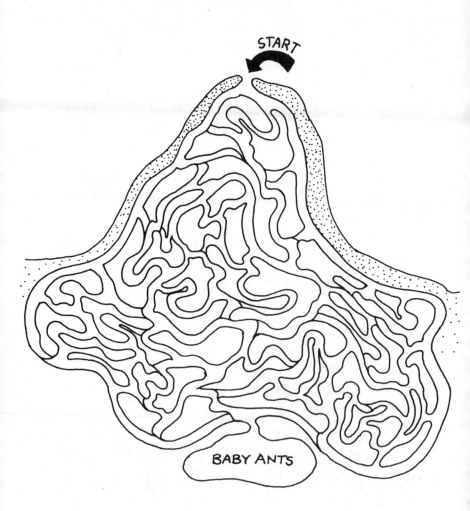

START

BABY ANTS

# Versigram

See if you can unscramble the following familiar Bible verses.

1. A oodg mane si ot eb rome seidder ahtn ergta cirseh, vafro si tebtre ahtn lsirev nad logd.

_____

_____

2. teL onahetr airspe oyu, nad ont uoyr won uotmh; a nsrtareg, nad ont uoyr won pisl.

_____

_____

3. peKe tcdeienpo dan iles arf mfor em, vige em tehinre vorepyt orn crihse; edfe em twhi het odfo htat si ym rotipno.

_____

_____

4. uBt eH rutend dna isda ot rePte, "eGt hbendi eM, tanSa! uYo rae a mustiblgn clbko ot eM; rfo uoy rea otn tenitgs uoyr ndmi no doGs tneiserst, ubt anms."

_____

_____

5. nl erveyhgtni I wosdhe oyu htta yb ikorgwn rhad ni htsi anrmne oyu stmu ephl het kawe nda emebrmre het roswd fo eht rLdo sJesu, ttha eH mHifesl adis, tl si erom dslebse ot vgei hnat ot ecviere.

_____

_____

# Key Word

To find the key word, fill in the blanks in words 1 through 10 with the correct missing letters. Transfer those letters to the correspondingly numbered squares in the diagram.

1. T ( ) E E        6. ( ) R C H

2. S W ( ) A T     7. ( ) I L E

3. ( ) A L E        8. S ( ) C K

4. T O W ( ) R     9. S T ( ) V E

5. S T O O ( )     10. S U ( )

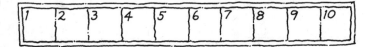

| 1 | 2 | 3 | 4 | 5 | 6 | 7 | 8 | 9 | 10 |
|---|---|---|---|---|---|---|---|---|----|
|   |   |   |   |   |   |   |   |   |    |

# Quotation Puzzle

In the puzzle below, fit the letters of each column into the boxes directly above them. The letters may or may not go into the boxes in the same order in which they are listed. It is up to you to decide which letter goes into which box. Once a letter is used, cross it off the bottom half of the diagram and do not use it again. Some letters have been entered into boxes to help you get started, and those letters have been crossed off. Black squares are used to separate the words of the quotation. When the diagram is filled in, you will find the completed quotation by reading the boxes horizontally.

# Alphagram

Twenty-six words from the Bible are hidden in the diagram below. See if you can find them all. There is one word in each row, and one letter is missing from each word. The missing letter may be at the beginning, end, or anyplace within the word. As you fill in the diagram, you will find that there are 26 missing letters—one letter for each letter of the alphabet. Since a letter will be used only once, an alphabetical listing has been provided for your assistance. As you use a letter in the diagram, cross it off the alphabetical list.

A B C D E F G H I J K L M N O P Q R S T U V W X Y Z

```
L  I  A  L  T  _  R  G  H  T  E
K  A  H  A  R  _  O  R  O  W  D
E  L  I  A  N  _  H  R  R  D  E
A  C  C  A  N  _  L  E  A  D  R
A  B  R  A  H  _  A  S  T  D  H
J  E  S  S  M  _  I  D  H  E  W
E  A  R  M  O  _  E  R  D  O  N
H  E  N  U  A  _  E  I  O  O  S
P  S  Q  O  A  _  L  W  G  D  T
R  E  C  A  N  _  E  N  E  H  L
S  O  H  M  W  _  I  S  T  S  Y
E  C  A  F  E  _  A  N  E  G  N
S  R  E  E  E  _  I  C  H  I  F
L  I  K  H  S  _  O  K  H  O  W
N  O  A  G  A  _  A  C  I  N  D
A  B  A  I  S  _  E  C  K  I  N
C  H  R  S  S  _  U  E  C  E  Y
E  A  S  L  U  _  A  N  E  M  D
P  O  B  A  A  _  P  H  A  S  Y
C  A  B  C  T  _  L  C  H  M  E
O  V  E  T  H  _  R  T  Y  E  D
C  A  P  R  I  _  I  N  D  E  H
S  A  R  L  O  _  O  A  P  E  M
M  E  F  A  B  _  S  S  E  H  O
B  A  N  A  B  _  S  S  N  H  M
M  A  B  A  Z  _  I  O  N  H  Y
```

# Name the Event

The picture below illustrates a Bible event, story, or verse.  See if you can guess which Bible event, story, or verse the picture is illustrating.

_____

_____

_____

_____

_____

Where in the Bible is this event, story, or verse found?

_____

# Something Is Missing

In six moves, see if you can discover the name of the one book in the Bible that does not contain the name of God.

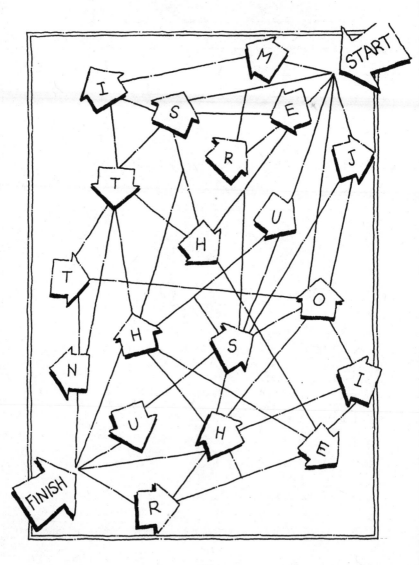

# New Testament Questions

1. _____ How long did it take for Herod to build his temple?

2. _____ After feeding the 5000, how many baskets of food were left over?

3. _____ How many wounds did Christ receive while on the cross?

4. _____ How long was Christ on the earth after His resurrection?

5. _____ How many were converted at the first sermon of Peter?

6. _____ What is the largest number of people converted at one time?

7. _____ How many deacons were appointed by the apostles?

8. _____ How many times is it recorded of Jesus standing at the right hand of God?

9. _____ How many instances of persons being stoned to death are recorded in the Bible?

10. _____ How many times does the Bible record people being put into prison?

A. 7

B. 46 years

C. 3000

D. 12

E. 9

F. 13

G. 5

H. 5000

I. 40 days

J. 7

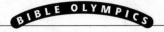

# Name the Event

The picture below illustrates a Bible event, story, or verse. See if you can guess which Bible event, story, or verse the picture is illustrating.

_____

_____

_____

_____

_____

Where in the Bible is this event, story, or verse found?

_____

_____

# Key Word

To find the key word, fill in the blanks in words 1 through 10 with the correct missing letters. Transfer those letters to the correspondingly numbered squares in the diagram.

1. ( ) E D
2. O L ( ) V E S
3. P H A ( ) I S E E
4. M I N I S ( ) E R
5. N A ( ) U M

6. ( ) O M E
7. M U S ( ) C
8. R E F U ( ) E
9. B A T ( )
10. M A N ( ) L E

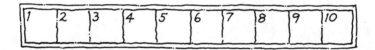

# Quotation Puzzle

In the puzzle below, fit the letters of each column into the boxes directly above them. The letters may or may not go into the boxes in the same order in which they are listed. It is up to you to decide which letter goes into which box. Once a letter is used, cross it off the bottom half of the diagram and do not use it again. Some letters have been entered into boxes to help you get started, and those letters have been crossed off. Black squares are used to separate the words of the quotation. When the diagram is filled in, you will find the completed quotation by reading the boxes horizontally.

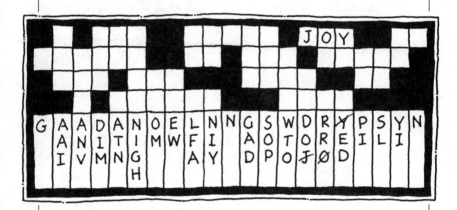

# Find the Rope

See if you can find the rope that the Philistines used to tie up the mighty Samson.

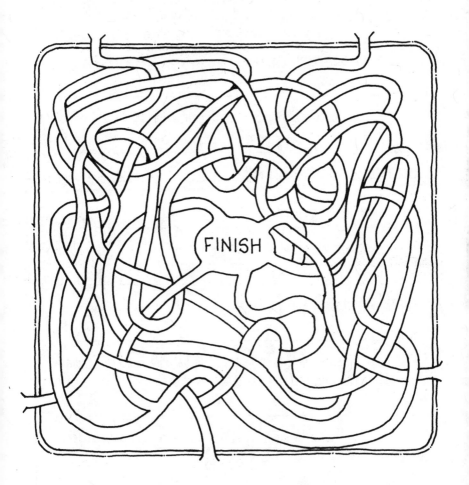

FINISH

# Who Said It?

All of the following quotes were said or written by one of the following men. See if you can guess "Who said it?"

### Matthew/Mark/Luke/John/Jude/Peter
### James/Paul/Gamaliel/Stephen

1. "For nothing is impossible with God."

_____

2. "A servant of Jesus Christ and a brother of James..."

_____

3. " 'Follow me,' he told him, and _____ got up and followed him."

_____

4. "Lord, do not hold this sin against them."

_____

5. "Then I saw a new heaven and a new earth..."

_____

6. "The people were amazed at his teaching, because he taught them as one who had authority, not as the teachers of the law."

_____

7. " 'A dog returns to its vomit,' and, 'A sow that is washed goes back to her wallowing in the mud.' "

_____

8. "But if it is from God, you will not be able to stop these men; you will only find yourselves fighting against God."

_____

9. "He is a double-minded man, unstable in all he does."

_____

10. "Avoid every kind of evil."

_____

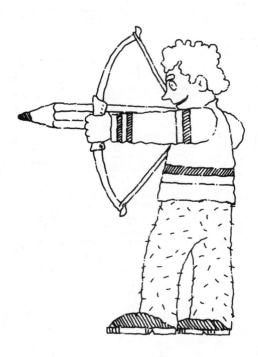

# Paul's Puzzle

Help Paul solve his puzzle by placing the 12 boxes, each containing one or two letters, into the empty diagram below. The puzzle will form four men's Bible names reading across and down, as shown in the small puzzle to the left.

# Bible Labyrinth

Hidden in the following Bible labyrinth is a verse from the Bible. Start with the entry arrow and move one space at a time to the right, left, up, or down. You should finish the verse at the exit arrow.

```
N O F G R Y R O T S E B A R R
A   F   A   B   H   H   Z   E
K B E N D E D X E C T D A G D
R   W   H   I   R   E   T   O
Y N U E R O M S I V K F E W G
I   M   L   J   K   I   S   L
E L D D O U S A R E L T O F A
A   I   M   E   S   R   E   C
T G N Y O U T U P J E S U S I
H   B   E   F   S   D   G   T
A H N L I K E C I T O I D O A
N   O   J   P   D   Q   K   D
A L F I E M A N D L O V E S E
F   I   D   Y   N   O   P   L
O R T Q C I T P U Z Z E L S Y
```

# Servant's Secret

Unscramble the mixed-up word below and see if you can discover
how we all should be.

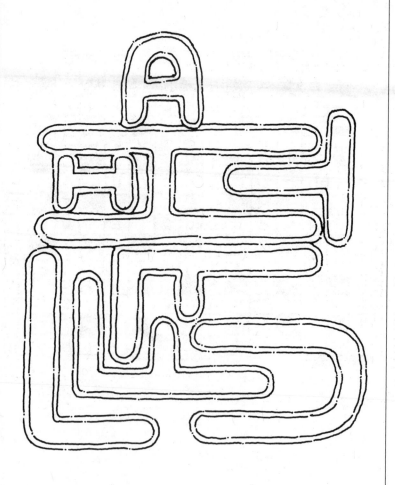

# Tail Tag

Begin at the bottom arrow and find a verse from the Bible. Move one square at a time to the right, left, up, down, or diagonally. End the verse at the top arrow.

| A | I | F | O | O | P | U | R | T | E | C | T | L | L | A | L | Y |
|---|---|---|---|---|---|---|---|---|---|---|---|---|---|---|---|---|
| Y | O | U | H | I | S | V | P | O | S | S | D | E | E | C | Z | T |
| T | H | I | O | T | G | N | S | K | N | A | E | E | N | I | S | S |
| H | O | L | O | I | J | I | Q | M | C | D | B | F | I | N | D | T |
| I | H | U | V | F | H | D | R | C | E | E | W | T | H | I | S | D |
| S | W | F | R | E | I | R | O | A | V | E | N | N | I | H | T | L |
| P | E | H | O | W | H | I | H | K | E | E | P | G | G | M | Y | L |
| U | Z | S | A | N | I | T | O | Y | D | O | G | S | I | I | N | A |
| G | P | U | O | Z | M | W | H | Z | W | L | E | S | L | T | A | Y |
| M | E | S | S | H | A | G | E | N | O | L | E | T | D | O | H | I |
| O | M | E | M | T | H | O | P | R | K | N | O | W | O | W | T | E |
| S | D | O | F | Y | O | U | K | A | N | D | I | N | W | I | L | L |
| T | O | W | I | N | I | S | E | N | O | L | K | L | Y | D | U | I |
| I | O | M | A | L | F | A | U | G | W | E | H | F | R | E | E | E |
| O | G | W | M | Y | O | I | T | D | H | B | O | D | K | M | I | E |
| F | H | E | H | T | R | A | U | E | N | A | H | A | U | E | G | R |
| W | R | I | T | T | E | N | E | A | T | A | N | O | T | E | S | T |

71

# Bible Men

The letters in the following columns go into the boxes directly below them, but in different order. When the letters are correctly placed, they will spell the names of eight Bible men. See if you can discover who these Bible men are.

| T | H | T | U | S | B | J | E | D | K | H | N |
|---|---|---|---|---|---|---|---|---|---|---|---|
| L | I | I | L | I | P | N | U | U | B | E |   |
| L | O | T | A | N |   | R | E | R | A | E |   |
| P | A | B |   | A |   |   | L | U |   |   |   |

# Old Testament Places

## A Difficult Challenge for the Expert

1. ____ Where did Cain go after killing Abel?

2. ____ To what mountain did Lot flee from Sodom?

3. ____ Where was Rachel buried?

4. ____ On what mountain did Moses speak to God?

5. ____ Where did Aaron die?

6. ____ From where did Moses view the promised land?

7. ____ At what place did the manna cease?

8. ____ At what place did Achan's sin first find him out?

9. ____ What cave was the hiding place of five kings?

10. ____ At what place did 70 kings have their great toes and thumbs cut off?

11. ____ What city was sown with salt by Abimelech?

12. ____ What is the name of Samson's birthplace?

13. ____ Where was the home of Goliath the giant?

14. ____ Where did Saul go to seek a witch?

15. ____ At what place did fire come down from heaven and consume 102 men?

A. **Endor**

B. **Nod**

C. **Gilgal**

D. **Samaria**

E. **Sinai**

F. **Bezek**

G. **Zoar**

H. **Shechem**

I. **Valley of Achor**

J. **Mosera**

K. **Gath**

L. **Nebo**

M. **Makkedah**

N. **Zorah**

O. **Bethlehem**

# Patchword

This patchwork-quilt diagram contains 10 Bible words or names all mixed up. Three patches form one word—use each patch only once. See if you can piece together the names and words and write them on the lines below.

1. _____     4. _____     8. _____

2. _____     5. _____     9. _____

3. _____     6. _____     10. _____

7. _____

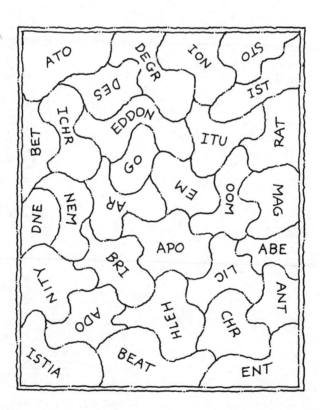

# Jumbles

For both of the jumbles below, unscramble the names of four men
mentioned in the Bible. Write these names on the blanks to the right.
The letters in the parentheses now form a new scrambled name. Write
these letters on the blanks provided. Now unscramble this name.

SCRAMBLED NAME          UNSCRAMBLED NAME

1. ZOAB                 ( ) __ ( ) __

   BENRUE               ( ) __ __ __ __ ( )

   BSAAMOL              __ ( ) __ ( ) __ __ __

   RCAESA               __ __ __ ( ) ( ) __

   New scrambled name   ( ) ( ) ( ) ( ) ( ) ( ) ( ) ( )

   Unscrambled name     __ __ __ __ __ __ __ __


2. EILAPT               __ __ ( ) __ __ ( )

   LESAI                __ __ ( ) __ ( )

   KKKAAUHB             __ __ ( ) ( ) __ __ __

   ESUEMTHHAL           __ ( ) ( ) ( ) __ __ __ __ __ __

   New scrambled name   ( ) ( ) ( ) ( ) ( ) ( ) ( ) ( )

   Unscrambled name     __ __ __ __ __ __ __ __ __

# Humorous Bible Riddles

1. What city in the Bible was named after something that you find on every modern-day car?

---

2. When the ark landed on Mount Ararat, was Noah the first one out?

---

3. Which one of Noah's sons was considered to be a clown?

---

4. Which came first—the chicken or the egg?

---

5. What did Noah say while he was loading all the animals on the ark?

---

6. On the ark, Noah probably got milk from the cows. What did he get from the ducks?

---

7. What was the difference between the 10,000 soldiers of Israel and the 300 soldiers Gideon chose for battle?

---

8. Certain days in the Bible passed by more quickly than most of the days. Which days were these?

_____

9. Matthew and Mark have something that is not found in Luke and John. What is it?

_____

10. In the story of the good Samaritan, why did the Levite pass by on the other side?

_____

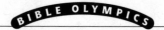
# Love Is an Activity

In I Corinthians 13:4-7, Paul talks about love being an activity. It is
something we do. The scroll has been rolled up so that you can't
read all the words. Can you finish the sentences without taking time
to unroll the scroll?

Love is p
Love is
It does
It does
It is n
It is no
It is not
It is no
It keeps
Love does
But rej
It alwa
Always
Always
Always
Love ne
Verse 13
And now
Faith, hop
But the
Is love

# Alphanumber

In the diagram below there are various numbers in each square. The numbers represent letters of the alphabet. Change the numbers to letters and discover an important Bible thought.

| A | B | C | D | E | F | G | H | I | J | K | L | M | N |
|---|---|---|---|---|---|---|---|---|---|---|---|---|---|
| 1 | 2 | 3 | 4 | 5 | 6 | 7 | 8 | 9 | 10 | 11 | 12 | 13 | 14 |

| O | P | Q | R | S | T | U | V | W | X | Y | Z | |
|---|---|---|---|---|---|---|---|---|---|---|---|---|
| 15 | 16 | 17 | 18 | 19 | 20 | 21 | 22 | 23 | 24 | 25 | 26 | 27 |

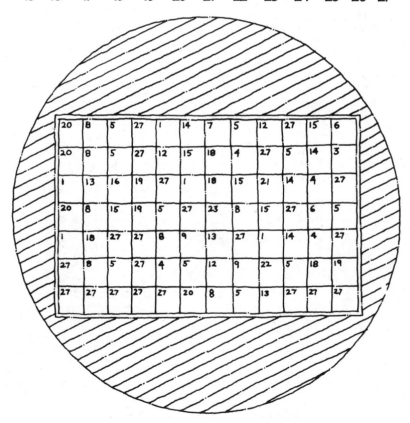

# Name the Event

The picture below illustrates a Bible event, story, or verse. See if you can guess which Bible event, story, or verse the picture is illustrating.

_____

_____

_____

_____

_____

Where in the Bible is this event, story, or verse found?

_____

_____

# Priscilla's Problem

Help Priscilla place the lettered pieces into the empty diagram below.
If placed correctly, 20 five-lettered words will be formed. The words
can be read by reading across the tops and bottoms of the pieces, and
by reading down the left and right sides of the pieces. The arrows
indicate where each word begins.

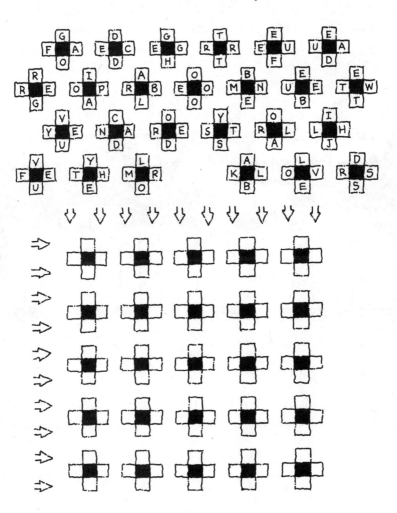

# Quotation Puzzle

In the puzzle below, fit the letters of each column into the boxes directly above them. The letters may or may not go into the boxes in the same order in which they are listed. It is up to you to decide which letter goes into which box. Once a letter is used, cross it off the bottom half of the diagram and do not use it again. One letter has been entered into a box to help you get started, and that letter has been crossed off. Black squares are used to separate the words of the quotation. When the diagram is filled in, you will find the completed quotation by reading the boxes horizontally.

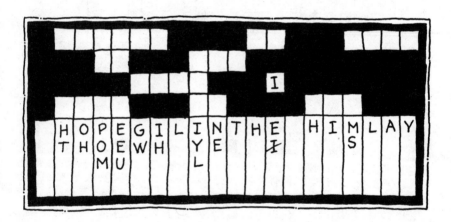

# Zebedee's Ziz-Zag

See if you can discover:

How many times the name Zebedee is used _____

How many "Z's" are in the puzzle _____

How many "E's" are in the puzzle _____

How many "B's" are in the puzzle _____

How many "D's" are in the puzzle _____

Be careful! The name Zebedee can run any direction in this puzzle.

```
Z  Z  E  B  E  D  E  E  Z  E  B  E  D  E  E
E  E  Z  B  Z  E  Z  D  Z  Z  Z  Z  E  E  Z
B  Z  E  B  E  D  E  E  E  E  E  E  Z  Z  E
E  E  B  Z  B  Z  B  Z  B  B  B  B  E  E  B
D  B  E  B  E  E  E  E  E  E  E  E  B  B  E
E  E  D  Z  D  B  D  B  D  D  D  D  E  E  D
E  Z  E  E  E  E  E  E  E  E  E  E  D  Z  E
Z  E  E  B  E  D  E  D  E  E  E  E  E  E  E
E  Z  E  B  Z  E  B  E  D  E  E  B  E  B  Z
B  Z  E  B  E  E  D  E  Z  E  E  B  E  E  E
E  Z  E  B  E  D  E  E  Z  D  E  D  E  D  B
Z  E  B  E  E  D  E  Z  E  B  E  D  E  E  E
E  Z  E  B  E  D  E  E  Z  E  B  E  D  E  E
Z  E  B  E  D  E  E  Z  E  B  E  D  E  E  D
E  Z  E  B  E  D  E  E  Z  E  B  E  D  E  E
```

# Help Moses

See if you can help Moses and the children of Israel find the
right path to the promised land.

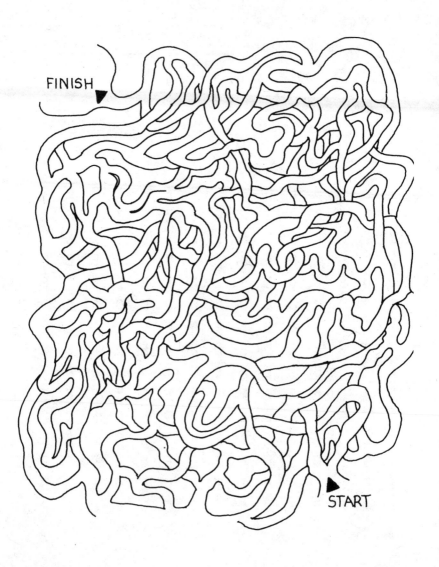

FINISH ▶

◀ START

# New Testament Challenge

1. _____ Who was reigning in Judah when Joseph returned from Egypt with the child Jesus?

2. _____ What prophet preached by the side of the river?

3. _____ Whose birthday was celebrated by dancing?

4. _____ Who was said to "strain at a gnat and swallow a camel"?

5. _____ Who was governor at the time of the crucifixion?

6. _____ Which apostle was a tax collector?

7. _____ Who was the man who carried the cross for Jesus?

8. _____ Who did the Lord strike dumb for not believing?

9. _____ Who issued a decree that the world should be taxed?

10. _____ What beggar was laid at the gate of a rich man?

11. _____ Who said "Nazareth! Can anything good come from there?"

12. _____ Who is reported as coming to Jesus by night?

13. _____ Who was appointed in the place of Judas?

14. _____ Whose face looked like an angel's while preaching?

15. _____ Who was struck blind when converted?

A. Matthew

B. Lazarus

C. Archelaus

D. Matthias

E. Nathanael

F. John the Baptist

G. Paul

H. Scribes and Pharisees

I. Stephen

J. Pontius Pilate

K. Nicodemus

L. Caesar Augustus

M. Herod

N. Zechariah

O. Simon

# Humpty Dumpty

In three moves, see if you can discover the name of a very fat man who
fell off his seat and broke his neck. The story is found in
1 Samuel 4:15,18.

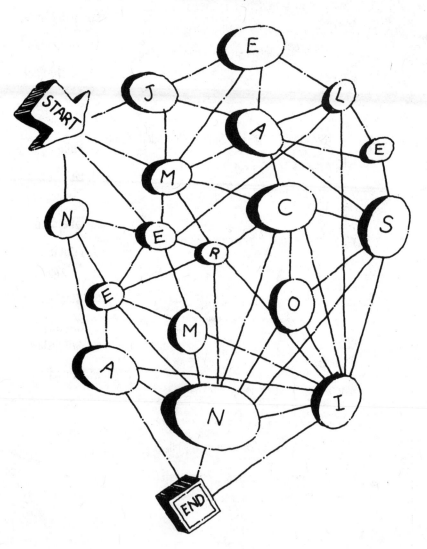

# Yachting with Noah

When Noah went into the ark it rained for 40 days and nights. Below, Noah has four opportunities to count the days, represented by four hexagons. There are six circles along the outside lines of each of the four hexagons. Can you place the proper numbers in the circles so that each hexagon totals 40? Six numbers have been placed in the circles to give you a head start.

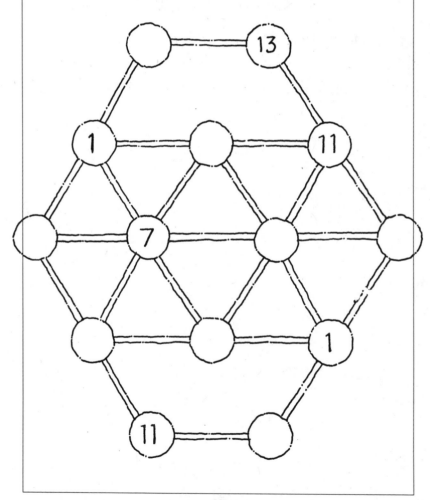

# Guess Who

Guess who the individual is that is mentioned. Match the proper person with the proper question.

1. _____Who was the inventor of string and wind instruments?

2. _____Who was the second oldest man in the Bible?

3. _____Who entertained angels unawares?

4. _____Who carried wood to the altar to burn himself?

5. _____Who was the youngest son of Jacob?

6. _____Who put his hand in his shirt and it became leprous?

7. _____Who was the father of Joshua?

8. _____Who said, "Be sure that your sin will find you out"?

9. _____Who was the king who had an iron bedstead?

10. _____Who was a left-handed judge that delivered Israel?

11. _____Who killed 70 of his brothers with one stone?

12. _____Who killed a lion at Timnah?

13. _____Who does the Bible say had six fingers on each hand?

14. _____Who killed the giant with 12 fingers and 12 toes?

15. _____Who killed a lion in a pit on a snowy day?

A. Benjamin

B. Ehud

C. Moses

D. Jared

E. Samson

F. Benaiah

G. Lot

H. Jonathan

I. Nun

J. A man from Gath

K. Jubal

L. Abimelech

M. Og

N. Isaac

O. Moses

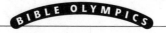
# Name the Event

The picture below illustrates a Bible event, story, or verse. See if you can guess which Bible event, story, or verse the picture is illustrating.

_____

_____

_____

_____

_____

Where in the Bible is this event, story, or verse found?

_____

_____

# Alphabet Fill-in

The 26 letters of the alphabet are missing from the puzzle below. See if you can place them where they belong. You can cross the letters off as you use them.

ABCDEFGHIJKLM

NOPQRSTUVWXYZ

# Peter's Race

Follow one continuous winding path to find a quote from Peter. The quote is found in 2 Peter 1:3. Start with the letter "H" and end with the letter "S." Each new word starts with one of the circled letters. The last letter of one word is next to the circled first letter of the next word. The number of letters in each word in the quotation is given below the answer blanks at the bottom of the page.

▼

```
Y D U R (H) O L I N E S S N D G O D J E S U S I
S H E E I P O R (L) I F E (A) B C D L I N E S S (T)
L V I (D) S O (F) L O V E S V L A L L M R U (O) H N
E I A T I X D E E O E (H) F (O) E G D A (K) T H G R
E N R R (H) A A (S) N O F I T H E S E I N N G U O
(P) O W E B S T (W) E V H M E H W V L W O O A G L
C H R I S G T (G) J L E (W) H O (C) Y L I T T L E O
D F N E V I O N C H I L D R A E N O S (B) Y (H) I
E G (U) K Z T H I O F K T H E L L E D (U) P I E S
L H S E A Y R L C R E N D O E Q I W O R L D (O)
I S (E) V E R T E S T S O H O U (A) Y R O L (G) N W
V E R S F R O M E S S I N (G) D N F O F G O D M
```

▼

| 3 | 6 | 5 | 3 | 5 | 2 | 10 |
|---|---|---|---|---|---|---|

| 2 | 4 | 3 | 4 | 3 | 9 | 7 |
|---|---|---|---|---|---|---|

| 3 | 9 | 2 | 3 | 3 | 6 | 2 |
|---|---|---|---|---|---|---|

| 2 | 3 | 3 | 5 | 3 | 8 |
|---|---|---|---|---|---|

# Answers

# Answers

## Page 1
### Name the Event

Saul watching the stoning of Stephen.

"And Saul was there, giving approval to his death."
—Acts 8:1

## Page 2-3
### Old Testament Time, Quantity, and Number

| | |
|---|---|
| 1. D—40 | 9. F—52 |
| 2. H—7 | 10. C—10 |
| 3. B—6 | 11. K—7 |
| 4. M—7 | 12. G—70 |
| 5. J—3000 | 13. A—7 |
| 6. G—70 | 14. E—70 |
| 7. A—7 | 15. I—40 |
| 8. L—7 | |

# Answers

## Page 4
### Runaway

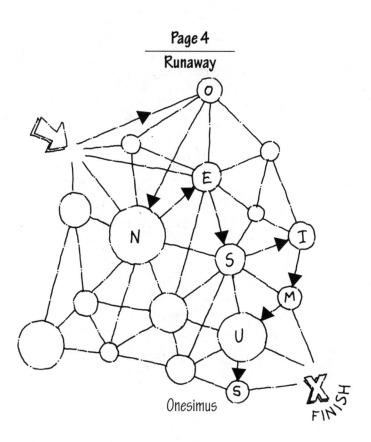

Onesimus

## Page 5
### Key Word

ANTICHRIST

# Answers

## Page 6
### Solomon's Treasure

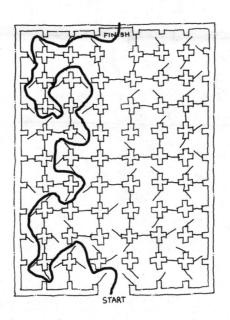

# Answers

## Page 7
### The Attributes of God

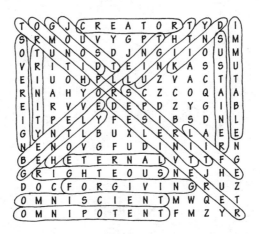

## Page 8
### Quotation Puzzle

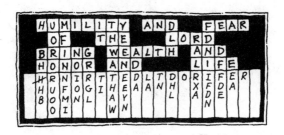

Proverbs 22:4

# Answers

## Page 9
### New Testament Questions

1. E—6
2. C—7 baskets
3. G—7 times
4. A—70 times 7
5. I—at the judgment

6. H—3 hours
7. F—2000
8. B—6 hours
9. J—7 years
10. D—3 1/2 years

## Page 10-11
### Who Said It?

1. Solomon—Song of Songs 6:6
2. Joshua—Joshua 1:8
3. Isaiah—Isaiah 6:8
4. Esther—Esther 7:3
5. Micah—Micah 5:2

6. Gideon—Judges 6:39
7. David—Psalm 91:1
8. Agur—Proverbs 30:28
9. Daniel—Daniel 5:16
10. Job—Job 28:28

# Answers

## Page 12
### Bible Labyrinth

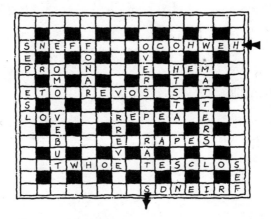

# Answers

## Page 13
### Patchword

1. ABRAHAM
2. ASSURANCE
3. BABYLON
4. BENJAMIN
5. CARPENTER

6. CREATION
7. GOMORRAH
8. HEBREWS
9. IDOLATRY
10. ISRAEL

11. JEZEBEL
12. OBEDIENCE
13. PHARISEES
14. SYNAGOGUE
15. TREASURE

# Answers

## Page 14
### Jumbles

| SCRAMBLED NAME | UNSCRAMBLED NAME |
|---|---|
| 1. KODAZ | ( Z ) A D O K |
| NIMJABEN | ( B ) ( E ) N J A M I N |
| GOABNEED | A B ( E ) D N ( E ) G O |
| EDSMA | ( D ) ( E ) M A S |
| New scrambled name | ( Z ) ( B ) ( E ) ( E ) ( E ) ( D ) ( E ) |
| Unscrambled name | Z E B E D E E |
| | |
| 2. HHAAORP | ( P ) H ( A ) R A O ( H ) |
| SUITT | T ( I ) ( T ) U S |
| PZORAH | Z O ( P ) H A ( R ) |
| DOBE | ( O ) B E D |
| New scrambled name | ( P ) ( A ) ( H ) ( I ) ( T ) ( P ) ( R ) ( O ) |
| Unscrambled name | P O T I P H A R |

# Answers

## Page 15

### Paul's Puzzle

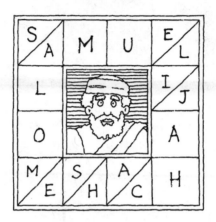

## Page 16-17

### Humorous Bible Riddles

1. The widow's "mite" and the wicked "flee"—Mark 12:42 (KJV) and Proverbs 28:1 (KJV).
2. Some people believe it was Zacchaeus. Others believe it was Nehemiah (Knee-high-miah), or Bildad the Shuhite (Shoe-height).
3. Because he went to the land of Nod—Genesis 4:16.
4. When God told Adam and Eve to go forth and multiply—Genesis 1:28.
5. When God divided the light from the darkness—Genesis 1:4.
6. His father was Enoch. Enoch never died; he walked with God—Genesis 5:24.
7. Yes. The duck took a bill, the frog took a green back, and the skunk took a scent.
8. In Proverbs 13:24 (KJV) — "He that spareth his rod hateth his son."
9. In Acts 1:14 (KJV) — "These all continued with one accord."
10. Elijah. He went up in a fiery chariot—2 Kings 2:11.

# Answers

### Page 18
### Versigram

1. "Be angry, and yet do not sin; do not let the sun go down on your anger"—
   Ephesians 4:26 (NASB).

2. "But godliness actually is a means of great gain, when accompanied by
   contentment"—1 Timothy 6:6 (NASB).

3. "Above all, keep fervent in your love for one another, because lover covers
   a multitude of sins"—1 Peter 4:8 (NASB).

4. "There is no fear in love; but perfect love casts out fear, because fear
   involves punishment, and the one who fears is not perfected in love"
   —1 John 4:18 (NASB).

5. "Do not fear what you are about to suffer. Behold, the devil is about to cast
   some of you into prison, that you may be tested, and you will have tribulation
   ten days. Be faithful until death, and I will give you the crown of life"
   —Revelation 2:10 (NASB).

### Page 19
### Fuzzy Thinking

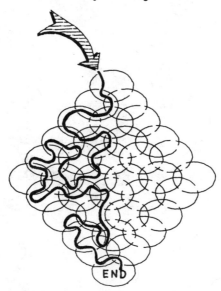

# Answers

## Page 20

### Alphanumber

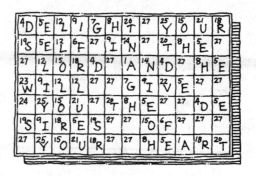

## Page 21

### Priscilla's Problem

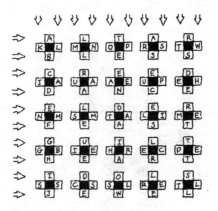

## Page 22

### Something You Should Be

TRUTHFUL

## Page 23

### Tail Tag

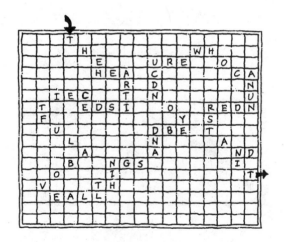

# Answers

## Page 24
### Name the Event

"And the prayer offered in faith will make the sick person well; the Lord will raise him up."
—James 5:15

## Page 25
### Quotation Puzzle

1 Samuel 16:7

# Answers

## Page 26

### Wrestling with a Lion

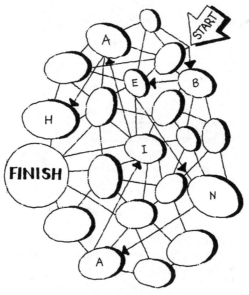

Benaiah

## Page 27

### Odd or Even

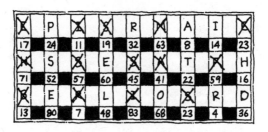

Praise the Lord!

# Answers

### Page 28

## 12 Things That Happen at Salvation

# Answers

## Page 29

### Old Testament Sprint

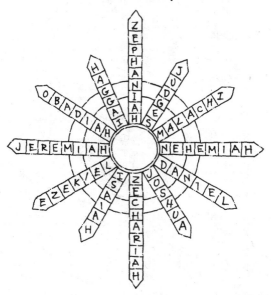

## Page 30

### Famous People Search

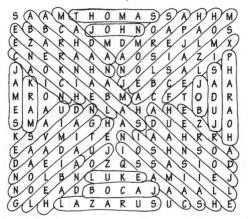

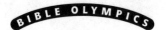

# Answers

## Page 31

### A Special Blessing

HOW BLESSED IS | THE MAN WHO DOES NOT WALK
IN THE COUNSE | L OF THE WICKED,
NOR STAND I | N THE PATH OF SINNERS,
NOR SIT IN | THE SEAT OF SCOFFERS!
BUT HIS DEL | IGHT IS IN THE LAW OF THE LORD,
AND IN HIS L | AW HE MEDITATES DAY AND NIGHT.
AND HE WILL | BE LIKE A TREE
FIRMLY PLAN | TED BY STREAMS OF WATER,
WHICH YIELD | S ITS FRUIT IN ITS SEASON,
AND ITS LEA | F DOES NOT WITHER;
AND IN WHAT | EVER HE DOES, HE PROSPERS.

## Page 32

### Odd or Even

| E | X | N | X | O | X | C | X | H |
|---|---|---|---|---|---|---|---|---|
| 14 | 17 | 2 | 1 | 64 | 39 | 72 | 73 | 10 |
| X | W | X | A | L | X | K | S | X |
| 41 | 24 | 89 | 52 | 46 | 27 | 4 | 36 | 11 |
| W | X | I | T | H | X | G | O | D |
| 8 | 93 | 22 | 12 | 38 | 81 | 44 | 18 | 66 |

Enoch walks with God.

# Answers

## Page 33

### Help Pharaoh

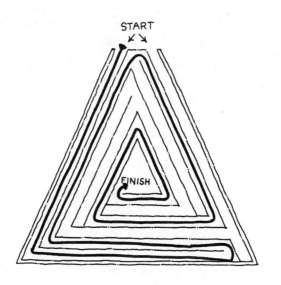

## Page 34

### Dodo's Dilemma

Number of Dodo's 207
Number of D's 127
Number of O's 128

# Answers

## Page 35
### Name the Event

Aaron and Hur held up the arms of Moses during the battle with the Amalekites. "When Moses' hands grew tired,m they took a stone and put it under him and he sat on it. Aaron and Hur held his hands up— one on one side, one on the other."
—Exodus 17:12

## Page 36
### Win First Prize

1. F—"Let there be light" (Genesis 1:3)
2. L—God (Genesis 3:21)
3. D—Cain (Genesis 4:17)
4. J—Lamech (Genesis 4:19)
5. N—Abraham (Genesis 22:3)
6. A—Sarah (Genesis 23:1)
7. H—Rebekah (Genesis 24:64, 65)
8. C—Moses (Exodus 18:13)
9. M—Aaron (Exodus 28:1)
10. B—Ananias (Acts 5:5)
11. K—Miriam (Numbers 12:10)
12. E—Saul (1 Samuel 31:4)
13. O—The widow at Zarephath's son (1 Kings 17:21,22)
14. G—Cornelius (Acts 10: 30-35)
15. I—Phoebe (Romans 16:1)

# Answers

## Page 37

### Nodding Off to Sleep

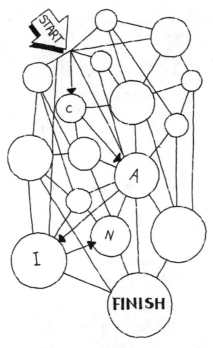

Cain

## Page 38

### Key Word

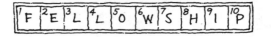

# Answers

## Page 39
### Quotation Puzzle

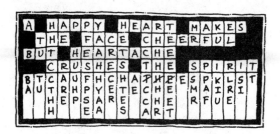

Proverbs 15:13

## Page 40
### Bible Labyrinth

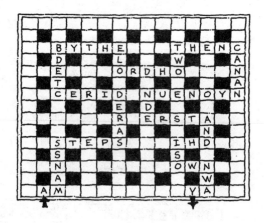

114

# Answers

## Page 41
### Patchword

1. COMMANDMENT
2. FIRSTBORN
3. EPISTLES
4. JUSTIFICATION
5. NAZARETH
6. OMNIPRESENCE
7. PERSECUTION
8. PHILISTINES
9. REDEMPTION
10. SOVEREIGNTY

## Page 42
### Jumbles

| SCRAMBLED NAME | UNSCRAMBLED NAME |
|---|---|
| 1. POHAR | O R ( P ) ( A ) H |
| IIRMMA | M ( I ) ( R ) ( I ) A M |
| OSLI | ( L ) O I ( S ) |
| CHJOEIAL | J E ( C ) O ( L ) I A H |
| New scrambled name | ( P ) ( A ) ( I ) ( R ) ( I ) ( L ) ( S ) ( C ) ( L ) |
| Unscrambled name | P R I S C I L L A |
| | |
| 2. LEBZEEJ | ( J ) ( E ) Z ( E ) ( B ) E L |
| SOARDC | ( D ) O R ( C ) A S |
| TVAIHS | V A S ( H ) T I |
| ONAMI | N A ( O ) M I |
| New scrambled name | ( J ) ( E ) ( E ) ( B ) ( D ) ( C ) ( H ) ( O ) |
| Unscrambled name | J O C H E B E D |

**115**

# Answers

## Page 43

### Name the Event

The woman accusing Peter and his denial. "But he denied it. 'Woman, I don't know him,' he said."

—Luke 22:57

## Page 44

### 28 Seasons

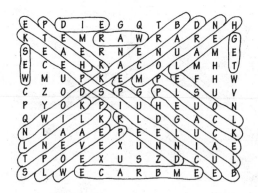

# Answers

## Page 45

### A Quote from John

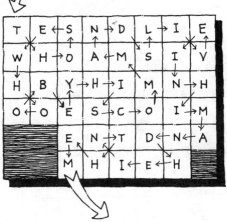

"Those who obey his commands live in him, and he in them."

## Page 46-47

### Humorous Bible Riddles

1. His equal—Isaiah 40:25; 46:5.
2. In Matthew 28:20 (KJV)— "Lo, I am with you always."
3. In Genesis 24:64 (KJV)— "Rebekah...lighted off the camel."
4. Is me. Isaiah said, "Woe, is me."
5. Grandparents.
6. Because her children had to play inside during the rain.
7. Fallen arches.
8. The Egyptians got a check on the bank of the Red Sea.
9. In 2 Kings 21:13 (KJV)— "And I will wipe Jerusalem as a man wipeth a dish, wiping it and turning it upside down."
10. He was a baker. We know this because he went to Philippi (fill-a-pie).

# Answers

## Page 48
### Odd or Even

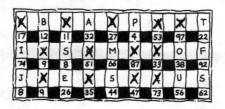

Baptism of Jesus

## Page 49
### Square Deal

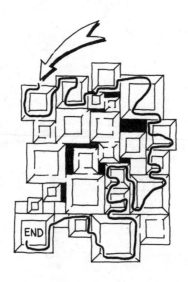

# Answers

## Page 50

### Bible Women

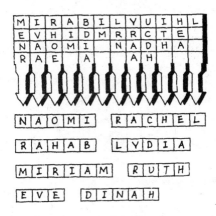

NAOMI    RACHEL

RAHAB    LYDIA

MIRIAM   RUTH

EVE    DINAH

## Page 51

### A Place for Everyone

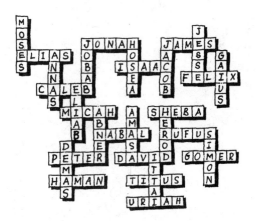

# Answers

## Page 52

### Extra Days

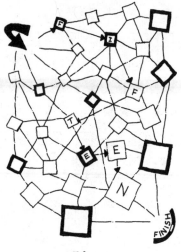

Fifteen

## Page 53

### Animals, Birds, & Reptiles

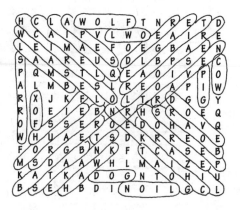

# Answers

## Page 54
### Help the Ants

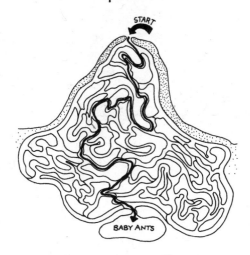

## Page 55
### Versigram

1. " A good name is to be more desired than great riches, favor is better than silver and gold"—Proverbs 22:1 (NASB).

2. "Let another praise you, and not your own mouth; a stranger, and not your own lips"—Proverbs 27:2 (NASB).

3. "Keep deception and lies far from me, give me neither poverty nor riches; feed me with the food that is my portion"—Proverbs 30:8 (NASB).

4. "But He turned and said to Peter, "Get behind Me, Satan! You are a stumbling block to Me; for you are not setting your mind on God's interests, but man's"—Matthew 16:23 (NASB).

5. "In everything I showed you that by working hard in this manner you must help the weak and remember the words of the Lord Jesus, that He Himself said, 'It is more blessed to give than to receive'"—Acts 20:35 (NASB).

# Answers

## Page 56
### Key Word

| ¹R | ²E | ³V | ⁴E | ⁵L | ⁶A | ⁷T | ⁸I | ⁹O | ¹⁰N |

## Page 57
### Quotation Puzzle

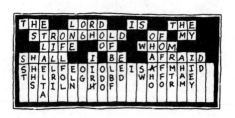

Psalm 27:1

# Answers

## Page 58

### Alphagram

```
          A    L    T    A    R         R
          H    A    A    B    O    R         R
               A    A    C    H    O    R
          C    A    N    D    L    E    T    H    D    O    N
                    H    E    A    R    S
                         F    G    I    E    D
     A    R    M    A    G    E    D    D    O    N
     N    O    A    H    I    E    S    W
     Q    U    A    J    L    E
                    K    E
          H    A    W    L
     C    A    M    E    M
               F    A    N    I    N    C    E
                    E    O    O    K    H
          A    G    A    P    A    E    N
                         Q    E    N    C    E    N
     A    S    S    U    R    U    H    E    E    M    Y
       B    L    A    T    A    P    C    E
       B    A    T    H    L    H
            C    T    I    R    C    H
     C    A    P    R    O    I    T    Y
     A    A    R    L    A
       F         A    B
               Y    S    S    O
               Z    I    O    N
```

## Page 59

### Name the Event

Job's comforters. "I have heard many things like these; miserable comforters are you all!"

—Job 16:2

123

# Answers

## Page 60
### Something Is Missing

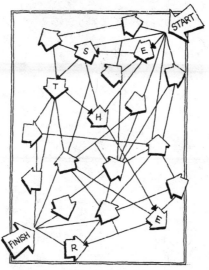

Esther

## Page 61
### New Testament Questions

1. B – 46 years
2. D – 12
3. G – 5
4. I – 40 days
5. C – 3000

6. H – 5000
7. A – 7
8. F – 13
9. J – 7 days
10. E – 9

# Answers

## Page 62
### Name the Event

Christ at the door. "Here I am! I stand at the door and knock.
If anyone hears my voice and opens the door, I will come in and eat with
him, and he with me."

—Revelation 3:20

## Page 63
### Key Word

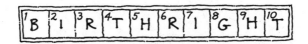

# Answers

### Page 64
---
### Quotation Puzzle

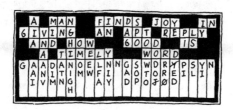

—Proverbs 15:23

### Page 65
---
### Find the Rope

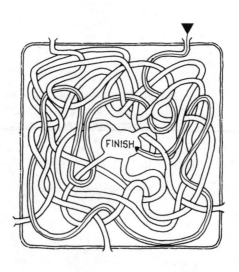

# Answers

## Page 66-67
### Who Said It?

1. Luke— Luke 1:37

2. Jude— Jude 1:1

3. Matthew— Matthew 9:9

4. Stephen— Acts 7:60

5. John— Revelation 21:1

6. Mark— Mark 1:22

7. Peter— 2 Peter 2:22

8. Gamaliel— Acts 5:39

9. James— James 1:8

10. Paul— 1 Thessalonians 5:22

## Page 68
### Paul's Puzzle

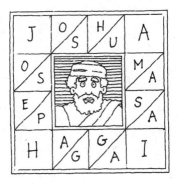

# Answers

## Page 69
### Bible Labyrinth

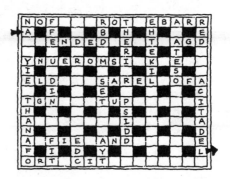

## Page 70
### Servant's Secret

FAITHFUL

# Answers

## Page 71
### Tail Tag

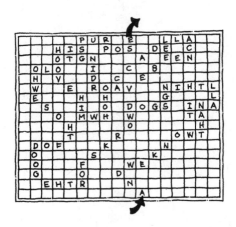

## Page 72
### Bible Men

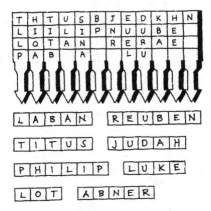

## Page 73
### Old Testament Places

1. B—Nod
2. G—Zoar
3. O—Bethlehem
4. E—Sinai
5. J—Mosera

6. L—Nebo
7. C—Gilgal
8. I—Valley of Achor
9. M—Makkedah
10. F—Bezek

11. H—Shechem
12. N—Zorah
13. K—Gath
14. A—Endor
15. D—Samaria

## Page 74
### Patchword

1. Abednego
2. Adoration
3. Antichrist
4. Apostolic
5. Armageddon

6. Atonement
7. Beatitudes
8. Bethlehem
9. Bridegroom
10. Christianity

# Answers

## Page 75

### Jumbles

| Scrambled Name | Unscrambled Name |
|---|---|
| 1. ZOAB | ( B ) O ( A ) Z |
| BENRUE | ( R ) E U B E ( N ) |
| BSAAMOL | A ( B ) S ( A ) L O M |
| RCAESA | C A E ( S ) ( A ) R |
| New scrambled name | ( B ) ( A ) ( R ) ( N ) ( B ) ( A ) ( S ) ( A ) |
| Unscrambled name | B A R N A B A S |

| | |
|---|---|
| 2. EILAPT | P I ( L ) A T ( E ) |
| LESAI | E L ( I ) A ( S ) |
| KKKAAUHB | H A ( B ) ( A ) K K U K |
| ESUEMTHHAL | M ( E ) ( T ) ( H ) U S E L A H |
| New scrambled name | ( L ) ( E ) ( I ) ( S ) ( B ) ( A ) ( E ) ( T ) ( H ) |
| Unscrambled name | E L I S A B E T H |

# Answers

## Page 76-77
### Humorous Bible Riddles

1. Tyre (tire).
2. He came forth out of the ark.
3. His second son.  He was always a Ham.
4. The chicken, of course.  God doesn't lay any eggs.
5. "Now I herd everything."
6. Quackers.
7. 9700.
8. The fast days.
9. The letter "a."
10. Because the poor man had already been robbed.

## Page 78
### Love Is an Activity

LOVE IS PATIENT,
LOVE IS KIND.
IT DOES NOT ENVY,
IT DOES NOT BOAST,
IT IS NOT PROUD,
IT IS NOT RUDE,
IT IS NOT SELF-SEEKING,
IT IS NOT EASILY ANGERED,
IT KEEPS NO RECORD OF WRONGS.
LOVE DOES NOT DELIGHT IN EVIL

BUT REJOICES WITH THE TRUTH.
IT ALWAYS PROTECTS,
ALWAYS TRUSTS,
ALWAYS HOPES,
ALWAYS PERSEVERES.
LOVE NEVER FAILS.
Verse 13
AND NOW THESE THREE REMAIN:
FAITH, HOPE AND LOVE.
BUT THE GREATEST OF THESE IS LOVE.

# Answers

## Page 79

### Alphanumber

| | | | | | | | | | | | |
|---|---|---|---|---|---|---|---|---|---|---|---|
| ²⁰T | ⁸H | ⁵E | ²⁷ | ¹A | ¹⁴N | ⁵G | ¹²E | ²⁷L | ¹⁵ | ⁶O | F |
| ²⁰T | ⁸H | ⁵E | ²⁷ | ¹²L | ¹⁵O | ¹⁸R | ⁴D | ²⁷ | ⁵E | ¹⁴N | ⁵C |
| ¹A | ¹³M | ¹⁶P | ¹⁹S | ²⁷ | ¹A | ¹⁸R | ¹⁵O | ²¹U | ¹⁴N | ⁴D | ²⁷ |
| ²⁰T | ⁸H | ¹⁵O | ¹⁹S | ⁵E | ²⁷ | ⁶W | ⁸H | ¹⁵O | ²⁷ | ⁶F | ⁵E |
| ¹A | ¹⁸R | ²⁷ | ²⁷ | ⁸H | ¹³I | ¹³M | ²⁷ | ¹A | ¹⁴N | ⁴D | ²⁷ |
| ²⁷ | ⁸H | ⁵E | ²⁷ | ⁴D | ⁵E | ¹²L | ⁹I | ²²V | ⁵E | ¹⁸R | ¹⁹S |
| ²⁷ | ²⁷ | ²⁷ | ²⁷ | ²⁷ | ²⁰T | ⁸H | ⁵E | ¹³M | ²⁷ | ²⁷ | ²⁷ |

Psalm 34:7

## Page 80

### Name the Event

The spies returning from the promised land.
"They cut off a branch bearing a single cluster of grapes. Two of them carried it on a pole between them."

—Numbers 13:23

# Answers

## Page 81

### Priscilla's Problem

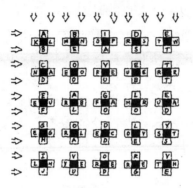

## Page 82

### Quotation Puzzle

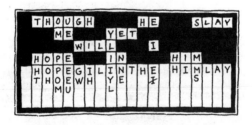

Job 13:15

# Answers

## Page 83
### Zebedee's Ziz-Zag

| | |
|---|---|
| How many times the name Zebedee is used | 31 |
| How many "Z's" are in the puzzle | 35 |
| How many "E's" are in the puzzle | 121 |
| How many "B's" are in the puzzle | 37 |
| How many "D's" are in the puzzle | 31 |

## Page 84
### Help Moses

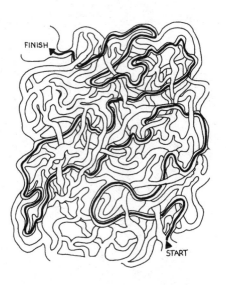

# Answers

---

### Page 85
### New Testament Challenge

1. C—Archelaus
2. F—John the Baptist
3. M—Herod
4. H—Scribes and Pharisees
5. J—Pontius Pilate
6. A—Matthew
7. O—Simon
8. N—Zechariah
9. L—Caesar Augustus
10. B—Lazarus
11. E—Nathanael
12. K—Nicodemus
13. D—Matthias
14. I—Stephen
15. G—Paul

---

### Page 86
### Humpty Dumpty

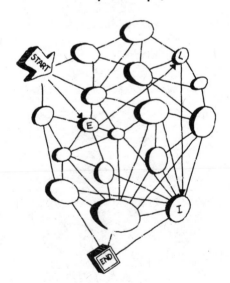

Eli

# Answers

## Page 87
### Yachting with Noah

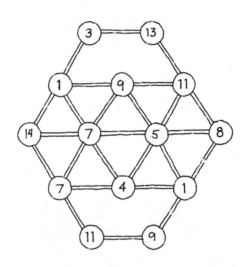

## Page 88
### Guess Who

1. K—Jubal (Genesis 4:21)
2. D—Jared (Genesis 5:18)
3. G—Lot (Genesis 19:1,2)
4. N—Isaac (Genesis 22:6)
5. A—Benjamin (Genesis 35:18)
6. O—Moses (Exodus 4:6)
7. I—Nun (Numbers 14:6)
8. C—Moses (Numbers 32:23)
9. M—Og (Deuteronomy 3:11)
10. B—Ehud (Judges 3:15)
11. L—Abimelech (Judges 9:5)
12. E—Samson (Judges 14: 5,6)
13. J—A man from Gath
     (2 Samuel 21:20)
14. H—Jonathan (2 Samuel 21:21)
15. F—Benaiah (2 Samuel 23:20)

# Answers

## Page 89

### Name the Event

The ravens feeding Elijah at the brook in the Kerith Ravine before the drought.

—1 Kings 17:1-4

## Page 90

### Alphabet Fill-in

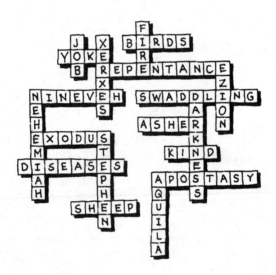

# Answers

## Page 91

### Peter's Race

| HIS | DIVINE | POWER | HAS | GIVEN | US | EVERYTHING |
|---|---|---|---|---|---|---|
| 3 | 6 | 5 | 3 | 5 | 2 | 10 |

| WE | NEED | FOR | LIFE | AND | GODLINESS | THROUGH |
|---|---|---|---|---|---|---|
| 2 | 4 | 3 | 4 | 3 | 9 | 7 |

| OUR | KNOWLEDGE | OF | HIM | WHO | CALLED | US |
|---|---|---|---|---|---|---|
| 3 | 9 | 2 | 3 | 3 | 6 | 2 |

| BY | HIS | OWN | GLORY | AND | GOODNESS |
|---|---|---|---|---|---|
| 2 | 3 | 3 | 5 | 3 | 8 |

## *Other Books by Bob Phillips*

WORLD'S GREATEST COLLECTION OF
CLEAN JOKES

THE RETURN OF THE GOOD
CLEAN JOKES

THE WORLD'S GREATEST COLLECTION
OF HEAVENLY HUMOR

THE WORLD'S GREATEST COLLECTION
OF RIDDLES AND DAFFY DEFINITIONS

THE WORLD'S GREATEST COLLECTION
OF KNOCK, KNOCK JOKES AND
TONGUE TWISTERS

THE BEST OF THE GOOD CLEAN JOKES

WIT AND WISDOM

HUMOR IS TREMENDOUS

THE ALL-NEW CLEAN JOKE BOOK

GOOD CLEAN JOKES FOR KIDS

THE ENCYCLOPEDIA OF
GOOD CLEAN JOKES

ULTIMATE GOOD CLEAN JOKES
FOR KIDS

AWESOME GOOD CLEAN JOKES
FOR KIDS

MORE AWESOME GOOD CLEAN JOKES
FOR KIDS

WACKY GOOD CLEAN JOKES FOR KIDS

NUTTY GOOD CLEAN JOKES FOR KIDS

LOONY GOOD CLEAN JOKES FOR KIDS

CRAZY GOOD CLEAN JOKES FOR KIDS

GOOFY GOOD CLEAN JOKES FOR KIDS

BIBLE BRAINTEASERS

THE GREAT BIBLE CHALLENGE

THE AWESOME BOOK OF
BIBLE TRIVIA

HOW CAN I BE SURE?

ANGER IS A CHOICE

REDI-REFERENCE

REDI-REFERENCE DAILY
BIBLE READING PLAN

THE DELICATE ART OF DANCING
WITH PORCUPINES

GOD'S HAND OVER HUME

PRAISE IS A THREE-LETTERED
WORD—JOY

FRIENDSHIP, LOVE & LAUGHTER

PHILLIPS' BOOK OF GREAT QUOTES &
FUNNY SAYINGS

THE ALL-AMERICAN QUOTE BOOK

BIBLE OLYMPICS

BIG BOOK—THE BIBLE—QUESTIONS
AND ANSWERS

THE UNOFFICIAL LIBERAL JOKE BOOK

WHAT TO DO UNTIL THE
PSYCHIATRIST COMES

---

For information on how to purchase any of the above books, contact
your local bookstore or send a self-addressed stamped envelope to:
Family Services
P.O. Box 9363
Fresno, CA 93702